DIGITAL FREEDOM

How Millions Are Carving Out a Dependable
Living Online, and How YOU Can Too

HUNG PHAM **MATT STONE**

www.digitalfreedom.academy

Published by:

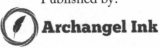 **Archangel Ink**

ISBN-13: 978-1-942761-79-2
ISBN-10: 1-942761-79-1

CONTENTS

LEARN MORE

Find this on Amazon, Audible, or other online vendors? Great! Be sure to visit our website to find out how we can help you succeed as an internet entrepreneur, freelancer, writer, instructor, consultant, and more.

Simply go to digitalfreedom.academy and join thousands of other freedom seekers.

Enjoy the book!

INTRODUCTION

Welcome freedom seekers. Hung Pham and Matt Stone here. We wrote this book because we're passionate about the freedoms that internet-based income has afforded us, and we know you can benefit from our insights and experience in your quest to achieve what we have.

Looking back at history, it's pretty obvious that humans have been on an ongoing journey to improve their lives—creating greater security, comfort, and freedom than the untamed natural world affords. That journey has been long and arduous and has undergone many phases. One theme seems to repeat itself again and again however, surfacing in many forms—from feudalism to slavery to the 21st century social stratification that now masquerades as "freedom." And that theme is one of a large working class supporting a small percentage of elites in their conquests for excessive power and wealth.

In every scenario, the lower class eventually revolts and forces change to take place. Comfort and security in exchange for unenjoyable or meaningless work can only satisfy a man for so long. Eventually, the desire to improve, the desire for progress, the desire for equality, the desire for autonomy, and ultimately the desire for freedom becomes too strong for the working class to bear.

We humans aren't good at being satisfied. We like working towards things, we like improving, we like to evolve and advance. The younger generations are no longer satisfied with a paycheck, food, clothing, and a roof overhead. We're humans. We yearn to get better. We never stop working towards it. We want more.

In today's day and age, "more" and "better" are represented by doing something enjoyable and meaningful with the bulk of our time. A better reality than what our parents and grandparents aspired to is one that involves greater time freedom, travel freedom, and work freedom. Improvement over the current status quo involves making more money in fewer hours. Better than working for someone else is working for yourself, creating your own vision as you see fit, and calling the shots.

The thing is, never before in human history have humans had more opportunities to make all of those major upgrades to their lives. With the power of the internet, millions are now carving out a dependable living for themselves, and they are doing so and typically making more money in less time. They're also typically having more fun and finding deeper meaning in what they do. And they are less tethered to a set schedule and a set location and can be more dynamic architects of their own lives.

This superior way of life isn't a foolish dream, it's our destiny as a species. It's what we've been working towards for millennia, and it's becoming a reality for countless individuals. Yet, so few believe that they too can join the digitally-free, or they don't understand just how easily and reliably money can be made online with the right approach.

And that's why we wrote this book. If you are seeking a better life—personally and professionally—we want to educate and inspire you to win the fight for your freedom. This book gives a good overview for those who find internet business to be daunting and mysterious. We hope to clear up confusion and simplify the process of going from beginner to winner online. We hope it builds your confidence, gives you some great ideas, and ultimately serves as a catalyst to transforming your life in ways you never thought possible.

Alright comrades, let's get started...

Part I
SEEKING DIGITAL FREEDOM

By Hung Pham

ABOUT ME

Hey there freedom seekers, I'm Hung Pham, the Chief Freedom Officer (CFO) of Digital Freedom Academy. Now before we get into the meat and potatoes of digital freedom, I want you to take a few minutes and clear your mind. Take everything you know about life, work—and everything in between—and toss it out the window.

Because today is the first day of the rest of your life. You are here for a reason. No, I'm not talking about here on Earth, I'm talking about this moment right now reading this book. You didn't accidentally stumble across it.

You downloaded this book because there was something in the title, cover, or book description that resonated with you. You've been carrying an emptiness for quite some time, and somewhere inside this book might lie the answer to give you a renewed sense of purpose.

You are here because you chose to be here. You are here because the words "digital" and "freedom" mean something to you other than an electronic clock and fireworks. It means waking up with a purpose every day and being in complete control of your life.

In high school, I got to see the rise of the Internet first hand and how it began to change the world. The Internet was revolutionizing so many industries that when I got to college, I studied computer science because I wanted to be part of that revolution.

Studying computer science wasn't enough for me because I was eager to learn more. I couldn't wait four years until I graduated to join the tech workforce. I needed to get involved NOW, and like a determined college student, I hustled my butt off for internships. Luckily for me, I got one at Sun Microsystems, which was one of the biggest tech companies at the time.

For those of you who aren't familiar with Sun Microsystems, getting an internship there is equivalent to working at Facebook or Google today. It was a reputable company to have on your resume. In 2004, I graduated and went on to work at Sun Microsystems full-time as an engineer.

Being in my early 20's and working at a company of that magnitude, my career was set for the next ten years or so I thought. But after my first two years working, I felt a change in me. It was getting harder to get up every day and come into the office. I started losing focus and began getting annoyed with the work I was doing.

It was hard to see the value of my efforts and what impact it made to the business. I didn't know it at the time, but I was slowly becoming a disengaged employee. I call it "The Working Dead" because every day when I was at work, I felt like a zombie.

What was once a tech powerhouse, Sun Microsystems began making a lot of business mistakes that they could never recover from. In 2009, it was bought out by Oracle and like that, a big brand was gone from the face of the Earth. How crazy would it be if Google or Facebook just suddenly vanished today?

As a result of the acquisition, I was laid off along with 75% of the company. For the first time in my life, I had no clue what I wanted to do. I only knew what I didn't want to do, but that wasn't good enough. I had to quickly find something to pay my bills and student loans.

I wound up taking various jobs at other big tech companies over the next few years because I needed to make money, but I was never happy. I had a six-figure salary but was slowly dying inside. I felt my life wasting away doing meaningless work. I was going crazy.

I know what you're thinking, "How can anyone with a six-figure salary complain about their job?" Well, $100,000 may seem like a lot to some people, but when you're living in Silicon Valley, that's barely enough to get by as a single person with no dependents. Forget about saving for a house and wedding.

Nobody understood me. I tried explaining to my parents once, but being typical Asian parents; they scolded me. The economy was going through a recession at the time, people were getting laid off left and right, it was hard to find work, and here I was complaining about my cushy high-paying Silicon Valley job.

Now in my early 30's, I couldn't fathom the thought that this was how the rest of my life would be. Wake up, go to a meaningless job, deal with corporate politics, go home, eat, sleep, rinse, and repeat. It was freaking depressing.

In my spare time, I would surf the web for hours reading about people who walked away from prestigious careers to find their own little piece of happiness. I remember thinking, "Wow! How can people walk away like that? How would they make money to survive?" And that's when I came across terms such as "passive income" and "nomadic lifestyle."

It was already impressive that these people were able to just get up and go; leaving behind everything they had worked hard for in their careers. But now they had new careers, ones that afforded them the luxury of living a new type of lifestyle. There was no such thing as 9 to 5 for these folks; everything was blended into one word—*life*.

It blew my mind that these people were finding ways to make a decent living on the internet while working just a handful of hours a week. "Was it even possible?" I thought. I became fixated on the notion of passive income, making money online, and being able to travel and work from anywhere in the world.

I even read about people who claimed to make anywhere from $10,000 to $50,000 a month. Was this true?

And if so, how could I do it, too?

How could I make more than $25,000 a month while only working 10 hours a week traveling the world with a beautiful babe in one arm and a mojito in the other? I had to know. I was determined to learn.

With my newfound purpose, my 9 to 5 job was now a means to an end. It paid the bills and nothing more. My real passion revolved around escaping the rat race on my way to being digitally emancipated. The internet became my new best friend.

Every day I spent hours upon hours in online forums only to be bombarded with people selling promises of a quick and easy payday with very little work involved. Like an old man on his last breath searching for the fountain of youth, I bought every product that came my way.

Now before we go any further, let me stop here and put out a disclaimer: There are tons of crap products out there on the internet. Predators are waiting to pounce on unsuspecting people preying on their weakness and desires.

Therefore, ALWAYS keep this in mind. If it sounds too good to be true, it probably is.

Yes, I bought a bunch of products that turned out to be garbage, and yes, I got very discouraged and almost gave up.

But I never stopped trying. Every time I bought a crappy product with false promises, I knew exactly what not to buy the next time around. I got smarter with what I was looking for and could easily spot shills.

Don't get me wrong. I was upset that I was wasting money on garbage, but I looked at it as getting my personal MBA. Instead of going to business school, I was getting real world business experience without the $100,000 school loan.

Eventually, I started to come across the right products and services that didn't make any big bold promises. They only focused on results. If it was a product on how to create a landing page, I learned how to create a landing page. If it was a product on how to get traffic, I learned how to drive traffic to my landing page. Nothing more, nothing less.

With all this fresh knowledge, I began to figure out all of the various complexities of the digital landscape. If I truly wanted digital freedom, there was a lot I needed to learn such as:

- Keyword research
- Search engine optimization
- Pay per click ads
- Email marketing
- List building

- Social media marketing
- Building landing pages and sales pages
- Copywriting
- Understanding marketing funnels

I know it sounds like a lot, and it is, but they all relate to one another. Once you learn one skill, it will make learning the next much easier. I soaked up as much knowledge as I could. I would read books, take courses, watch tutorials—anything that taught me what I needed to know to become digitally free.

But most importantly, I actually started DOING it and experimenting. Reading can only do so much. It's only when you take action that you learn the most, and that's when I finally made my breakthrough, which I'll explain more in the next chapter…

MY FIRST DIGITAL PRODUCT

My first venture into the world of entrepreneurship and digital freedom was an eBook I created on how to crate train puppies. What is crate training exactly? Well, if you've ever seen those metal cages that hold dogs and cats at a pet store, those are crates.

By crate training puppies, owners get them used to staying in a cage. I know it sounds cruel to put puppies in a cage, but this is convenient when nobody is home to watch them. The last thing a dog owner would want are puppies running around pooping everywhere and chewing on furniture.

Now, what made me qualified to write a book on this? What credentials did I have for puppy crate training? None to be honest. I love dogs, but I'm no Asian dog whisperer. I've never even owned a puppy in my life!

I created a digital product on crate training puppies because my keyword research showed an average of 33,000 monthly searches on Google for terms related to crate training puppies. What made it even better were the low competition for competing products that showed up on ads when you searched on Google.

With an average of 33,000 monthly searches on Google and few competing ads, I decided it was a good enough investment to create a digital product to sell on puppy crate training. An eBook was the easiest product I could create, launch, and test with little financial investment.

I would spend the next two weeks researching as much as I could on puppy crate training. Eventually, I produced a 10,000 word eBook ready to sell. Keep in mind that the content in the book was simply content I found in my research but paraphrased in my own language to ensure I wasn't plagiarizing.

Next, I published my eBook on Gumroad, a platform that allows creators to sell digital and physical products to consumers. I then bought a domain, created a long form sales page, wrote some pretty banging copy, and I was ready to rock and roll. All I needed now was some traffic.

Remember all the keyword research I did early on? I took those same keywords and created Google ads for them. This was how I planned on getting traffic to come to my sales page. It wasn't free, but it was the quickest way to get the traffic I needed in order to test.

I set up my ads and launched my eBook on a Saturday night. When I woke up the next morning, I made two sales for a total of $25. "Holy freaking shit!" I yelled. I did It, I created a digital product and made my first dollar. It was the most amazing feeling ever.

Over the next two weeks, I would only sell two more copies for a total of $55 in sales while spending over $200 in ads for a net loss of $145. It didn't matter because the experience itself was worth it. I got over that first hump. I was able to sell my first digital product. A $145 loss was a small price to pay for that monumental lesson.

I took the domain and sales page down shortly after because crate training puppies wasn't a business I wanted to be in nor was I passionate about it. I only did it to prove something to myself, which I did. It was the ultimate confidence booster.

If you wanna see what the actual eBook looks like, you can still view it here: gumroad.com/l/puppy-crate-trainer

Notice how I changed my name to Hunter Price. I thought having an Americanized name would give me more credibility as an author, HA!

The biggest takeaway from this entire experience that I can share with you is to just start somewhere. You don't need to wait until you have that perfect product or perfect business idea. Done is better than perfect. Get it out there, start testing, learn from your mistakes, iterate, and repeat.

While I'm nowhere near as experienced as Matt is (he'll be your guide through most of this book), I did want to provide a summary of the biggest lessons I've learned so far before passing the baton off to him. Let's do that next…

COMMON MYTHS AND MY BIGGEST LESSON

In this chapter, I'll go over the five biggest myths about digital freedom from my experience and the takeaways from my four years of being a digital entrepreneur.

Myth #1 – I'm Not Smart Enough

Sometimes I hate the way the media glamorizes digital entrepreneurs, especially when they use clickbait titles for their articles like this one:

"This 21-year-old dropped out of college and started a business last year and is on track to earn 1 million dollars."

What do I normally do when I come across these headlines? I click, and I read them of course; that's what these headlines were meant to do. They are written in a way that teases at your curiosity and desires.

The problem with these headlines is that they create a sense of "us" vs. "them." It creates a mental divide where you begin to worship these digital entrepreneurs as if they are the next Steve Jobs when they're not.

I'm not knocking on anyone's hustle and success. That's the last thing I would ever do. What I hate is how the media portrays the success. The truth is that these people who quit their jobs and are now making a decent living online are no different from you and me.

They are regular folks who at one point in their lives wanted something more than the typical 9 to 5. They started their digital careers from the same starting point as the rest of us and eventually built it into something sustainable.

They are no smarter than us. I would even argue that we are smarter than some of them. What makes them successful is that they continue to work at their craft with persistence and resilience.

Famous billionaire entrepreneur Mark Cuban has a term for this called "sweat equity." When you start off creating a business, you have very little money, resources, and capital.

The only thing you have an abundance of is your sweat equity; aka your time and effort. If you're not willing to put in the work to make your dreams come true, then who else is going to do it?

The next time you come across an article that puts digital entrepreneurs on a pedestal, don't feel like you are incompetent. Remember that these entrepreneurs are ordinary people, who, with a little bit of luck, put in the time and effort to make it happen.

Myth #2 – I Can't Start Until I Have the Perfect Idea

Repeat after me:

"Done is better than perfect."

"Done is better than perfect."

"Done is better than perfect."

From this day forward, promise me that you'll ingrain that phrase into your memory. If you want to succeed as a digital entrepreneur, you have to get comfortable with being done instead of being perfect.

The reason why this is crucial is that perfect is subjective. What is perfect to me may not be perfect to you and vice versa. When you are stuck on trying to be perfect, you aren't making progress, and without progress there is no accomplishment.

When you can get something done or about 75% of the way to what you consider perfect, that's good enough to launch and see what kind of results you get. The data you get from testing is critical to your success.

There is no such thing as getting it right on the first try. Too often people wait until they have the perfect domain, the perfect logo, the perfect copy, the perfect color scheme, the perfect image—and then they launch.

Wanna guess what happens next?

Absolutely nothing. Zilch, zero, nada, sayonara. No sales, no users, no downloads, no money, no nothing. I've seen people spend tons of money and time to launch a product only to wonder why they can't get any buyers.

Then when it turns out that they created a product that nobody wants, they become so emotionally attached to it that they refuse to change course—spending more time and money trying to fit a round peg into a square hole.

Had they just got something decent enough to launch, they could've easily figured out whether the product was desirable and make corrections as needed. I'm a big proponent of testing. I test everything when it comes to creating and selling digital products.

I test my email subject lines. I test how I format my emails. I test the color scheme on my landing pages. I test where to insert my call to action on my landing pages. I obsess over testing, and it's because of that, I've found success as a digital entrepreneur.

Stop worrying about being perfect and just focus on being done. Only when you're done enough to put something out there does the process of really figuring out how to succeed begin.

Myth #3 – I Can't Afford to Quit My Job, It's Too Risky

Hey, I get it. This dream of being digitally free is nice, but it's hard to commit to if you gotta worry about the roof over your head and putting food on the table. But check this out, nobody said you needed to quit your job to chase your dreams.

In fact, I would argue against that. You shouldn't quit your job to chase this dream. Instead, you should keep your job and work on your dream in your spare time until you can get to a level where you financially feel comfortable enough to quit your job.

That is the smart thing to do.

Working towards digital emancipation is tough. I know it's called passive income, but there is very little that is passive about it. It's a lot of work, energy, and sweat. You could do 90% of the things required correctly, but that missing 10% will somehow find a way to screw you up.

Which is why you shouldn't quit your job. The added stress of not having a steady paycheck isn't worth it. Instead, you should keep your job and start a few side projects purely as a learning experience.

When I started on this digital journey four years ago, I had no clue what I was doing. I had some idea on how to get started but no concrete blueprint laid out for me. By keeping my job, it allowed me to experiment and learn until things made sense.

In my own experience, having side projects made my crappy job more bearable. Let me explain why. Before I started dabbling in digital entrepreneurship, all I knew was my 9 to 5 job. That's the only career I had.

Every day I got up at 6:30 am to get ready for a job I had absolutely no passion for. After showering, getting dressed, and eating a quick breakfast, I spent approximately an hour each morning in soul-sucking traffic on the way to work.

Once I was at work, it was a game of figuring out how to survive for the next eight hours without poking my eyes out with a pen before I got the luxury of another hour-long commute home in traffic.

I freaking hated my job. Did I mention that already?

However, once I started dabbling in a few digital side projects, work wasn't that bad anymore. Work didn't change. I still had the same tasks and responsibilities, but it was my mindset and mentality that changed.

I had a newfound purpose and career trajectory. Work was now a means to an end. It paid my bills so that I could continue working towards my digital freedom. There was nothing more to it. When I saw that I had options in my career, I had a much more positive outlook on life. I had something to work towards. I had something positive to stay focused on instead of feeling trapped with no idea how I could escape.

In short, don't quit your job mainly for two reasons:

The added stress of not having a steady income can be distracting to your learning. Of course, if you have a good amount of money tucked away that you can afford to live off of, then, by all means, quit your job if you hate it.

Having a job while you work on side projects can benefit your learning. Instead of worrying about making it work, you can focus on what you learned from each experiment and make the next one better.

Myth #4 – I Can't Do It Because Someone Else is Already Doing It

I have an older cousin named Mark. Mark is a pretty chill guy who enjoys traveling and loves working out. He is interested in the idea of traveling the world and working from a beach bungalow, but he isn't sure how to make it happen. He's only read about people living this life.

Every time I see my cousin, I always encourage him to do something in the fitness space because he's a fitness junkie. His response to me is always, "Someone's already doing it."

Yes, dear cousin I know that, but work with me for a minute and open your mind up to a new way of thinking. Facebook is the largest social network in the world, and it isn't the first or even the second social network to become a global phenomenon.

Remember Friendster? They were first on the scene, but because of the poor technology it was built on, they couldn't keep up with the explosive growth. They lost users as quick as they gained them once the site performance slowed to a halt.

What about MySpace? They were dominant for a while. In the spring of 2008, MySpace was still top dog when it came to social networks. However, that April, a teeny tiny startup by the name of Facebook took over the lead and never looked back.

How did that happen? How did the once-dominant MySpace fall from grace? Simple, they failed to innovate their core product. MySpace was created by people in the entertainment industry and not by technology gurus.

Which is why when it came time to innovate, MySpace did not have the talent to quickly fend off rival upstarts. Facebook provided users with a better and improved way to engage online, and that was the end of MySpace.

There are two very important lessons I want you to take away from this example:

The first lesson is about being first to market. Being first doesn't mean that you dominate the market. Regardless of whatever industry you are in, being first just means you are first to arrive.

There is no guarantee that you will dominate your market and even if you are dominating your market, being first doesn't guarantee that you will stay that way forever.

The second lesson goes hand in hand with the first lesson. You need to continuously innovate your product, your service, whatever it is you are selling to customers. If you cannot innovate and evolve, you will die. If you don't innovate, somebody else will and you'll get left behind.

This is as simple as human evolution.

The next time you have an idea for your business, don't worry if someone else is already doing it. In fact, the more people in your space the better because it shows that there is a market. Instead, look at your competitors and see how you can do it differently, serve a different demographic, offer better value, or just plain do it better than they can.

Myth #5 – I Don't Have the Time Right Now

I've come across many people who supposedly want to achieve digital freedom, but when I ask them about what progress they have made thus far I get one very simple answer: "I haven't started yet, I don't have the time right now."

I think to myself, "Okay, we all have busy lives." I then ask them when would they be able to start, and they say, "I don't know yet, soon hopefully." As soon as I hear those words, I know they're not serious. I also know they won't ever be digitally free. They don't make it a priority.

Let me remind you that this is your life that you are living. If you don't make your dreams come true, then who is going to do it? It's certainly not Matt or me. We can write books, create courses, and even offer personal mentorship, but at the end of the day, if you don't make the time to put in the effort, change won't happen.

I used to think I was busy until I actually tracked my daily activities for an entire month. I was surprised to see how much time I actually waste on things that aren't necessary.

Surfing the web, Facebook, watching TV… I was guilty of all these offenses. I thought I was busy, but I wasn't. It only seemed like I was busy because I was bored, but after seeing on paper how much time I wasted on these activities, I knew I had to make some changes.

I surfed the web only if it was necessary and limited how much time I spent on Facebook. I cut out TV completely because it wasn't something I needed on a daily basis. I then created a new schedule where I forced myself to spend an hour or two each day on my side projects.

To be honest, I didn't even miss TV or Facebook once I got started. My side projects consumed all of my attention, and I found, just as Matt has, that time spent working on something constructive is more fulfilling than any entertainment could ever be. An hour or two daily quickly became four or more. The best part was that none of this ever seemed like grunt work. I was teaching myself new skills and the more time I put into it, the quicker I picked up these skills.

To take it a step further, I began to create deadlines for myself. If I was learning how to set up a landing page, I would give myself a deadline of a week to get it done. This lit a fire under my butt and really forced me to be super productive with my time.

I highly recommend putting a deadline on anything you do, even if you aren't sure you can hit the deadline. By having a deadline, you are mentally forcing yourself to take action.

You ever have that friend that's always talking about doing something big "one day?" I have a few friends like that, and the sad part is that I already know they'll never get around to doing that big thing.

When you say words like "one day" or "someday," you are essentially leaving yourself an out. You're conditioning yourself to think that it's okay to procrastinate because "one day" and "someday" will always be there.

It's dangerous to have this kind of mentality because you get stuck in this cycle of wanting to do something but putting it off because you'll get to it one day. You have more time than you think. Put a deadline to it and start working.

There you have it, the five biggest myths when it comes to digital freedom and my biggest takeaways. I've learned a lot the last four years on this journey, and I'm still learning every day. While I can sit here and talk about this subject for hours, my recommendation for you is to get started.

As soon as you finish this book, get started—even if you have no clear idea on what you want to do. You can plan all day long, but it only matters when you execute. It's okay to fail, but it's not okay to give up.

I wish I could share more, but I'm right in the midst of putting on my annual Culture Summit in San Francisco. I'll have to turn it over to Matt now. Pay close attention, as Matt has an incredible wealth and breadth of experience online. By the time he's through, you should have an amazing overview of how money is made online and a clearer vision for how you can turn your own talents and interests into something potentially viable as an internet-based career.

Enjoy. Hope to see you over at Digital Freedom Academy…

Part II
WHAT IS DIGITAL FREEDOM?

By Matt Stone

ABOUT ME

So who am I and what makes me qualified to write a book about digital freedom? I'm Matt Stone, digitally-free since 2011. I'm perhaps the most freedom-obsessed human on earth, and I've got a vast variety of experience in earning money online that includes: blogging, self-publishing, freelancing, email marketing, vlogging, podcasting, network marketing, subscriptions, teaching, coaching, consulting, and more.

About the only major form of internet moneymakin' that I haven't dabbled in is the sale of physical products, but I've still received a ton of exposure to that world as my father sells products through Amazon and can hardly carry a conversation about anything else. He loves it.

It's quite a rap sheet looking back at all that I've done. Don't get the wrong idea about me though. I'm not one of those money-obsessed hucksters trying to "hack" the interwebz for my own personal gain. I didn't get started online to become a millionaire. I didn't start out because I'm a douchebag who's all about being one of those yuppie entrepreneurs. In fact, I still cringe a little at the word "business." It's not who I am at all.

I'm not even an advocate of personal wealth. I think personal wealth is a disease that affects individuals and society in a profoundly negative way. The whole idea of it is a selfish, consumerism-driven fantasy. Despite running a business that hauls in almost 7-figures annually, I and my two lovely dependents live off of just $3,000 per month. We try to keep the luxurious expenditures to a reasonable minimum. We'll see the inside of a tent more than 100 nights on the long summer trip we're currently on (I'm literally typing this at campsite 7 at the Pacific Creek campground just outside of Grand Teton National Park).

Rather, I seek freedom and a life filled with adventure, passion, experiences, and ultimately fulfillment. And, having achieved that pretty gloriously, it's REALLY fulfilling to help others do the same. It takes a lot of personal restraint not to run up to every 9-5 employed person I meet, shake them violently, slap them in the face, and shout, "Whhhhyyyyyyy??!!"

My dedication to freedom didn't begin with the internet though. My search for freedom from the shackles of employment pre-dates my digital experiences by more than a decade.

I did most of my growing up near one of the world's meccas for wealthy tourists—where women instinctively flock like the salmon of Capistrano. Where Lloyd and Harry set out to return a briefcase to Mary Samsonite. I'm talking about a little place called Aspen.

It was here that a little seed sprouted in my relatively-empty 17-year old head. Observing the relationship-ruining workaholism of my father while simultaneously being surrounded by hordes of people that were all on vacation, I wondered to myself, "Why not strive to ALWAYS be on vacation?"

I also wondered why people who could afford $10,000 per night hotel rooms and fur-coat wearing, diamond-knuckled, fake-breasted housewives were lucky to be able to get away from work for a whole week at a time.

I didn't envy them in the slightest, and set out to measure my own personal wealth in annual vacation time.

And so, for the next ten years, I had one massive adventure after another. Even the "work" I did was an adventure.

I "worked" as a Wilderness Ranger doing my absolute favorite thing on earth (hiking) for 7, 4-month seasons.

I travelled the country working at the best restaurants I could for a few months at a time when I wasn't on vacation or working as a Ranger. It took me to places like a remote fishing lodge in Alaska and Napa Valley. In the process I became an extremely knowledgeable and talented chef. I could have had a very successful career if I gave a shit about careers, haha.

I lived in Jackson Hole, Wyoming where I took a whole winter off to ski and write a book (that was crappy and that I never published).

I travelled to Nepal to trek the Himalayas.

I travelled all over Japan and Southeast Asia.

I went to Central America where I learned Spanish (much of it forgotten now, please don't write to me in Spanish!).

I spent three winters in Maui. Yes. Maui.

I took tons of huge road trips, went on countless big treks in the Wilderness, and skied until my shins and back hurt too bad to ski anymore.

All in all, I worked for an average of about six months per year after graduating college, and even while I was in college I took semesters off to travel and ski, and hopped around from college to college in cool places like Bozeman, Montana and Boulder, Colorado.

The other six months per year were spent recreating, doing something creative, or otherwise doing something that seemed really cool to me at the time.

Basically what I'm saying is that I was Tim Ferriss before Tim Ferriss was Tim Ferriss. I didn't even need to go to an Ivy League school, start a business, and work myself into the ground to figure out that time, adventure, purposeful projects, and freedom are the ultimate forms of wealth.

The thing is though, it's not just me who revolted against the career and consumerism-driven norms of society. Many of the 59 people I graduated high school with forged similar paths for themselves. I think many of us saw the people who came through Aspen—the supposed elite, accomplished rulers of society—and we didn't like what we saw. At all. Most of them couldn't even ski. They were just there to say they were there.

When I was in Maui, about 10% of my graduating class was there as well. Just for the heck of it. Because Maui is cool and playing in the ocean is fun.

I just found out one of my classmates is the first woman to ever float the entire Amazon river solo. Go Darcy!

I tell you all this because living your life in pursuit of freedom above wealth, career, accolades, boats and hoes—or whatever seems to drive the choices of most modern North Americans—isn't hard or anything. It's easy to do—much easier than winning the rat race for sure.

It reminds me of the movie *Office Space* when the main character declares that if he had a million dollars he would literally do nothing all day, and his neighbor replies with something like, "Well hell man, you don't need a million dollars to do that." Achieving a freer lifestyle isn't something that is difficult to do. It's right under your nose, you just don't realize it.

It's also a choice. It's a mindset. And that mindset is one shared by many of the people I grew up with precisely because we got to witness the lifestyles and attitudes of the world's wealthiest people. Any fantasies we had about being multi-millionaires or big dick playa CEO's or whatever was shattered. We came out of that place with a different value system—one built around living a full, rich life first and foremost above material wealth. At least, I feel like most of us did. It wasn't just me. I'm not that special.

Hopefully in this book I can somehow help you catch the Freedom bug. It's a great way to live. And the digital age has brought us freedom seekers an unprecedented abyss of new opportunities. I'd love to give you an overview of how many opportunities there are, and show you just how simple and straightforward it can be to carve out a reliable income for yourself that is completely location-independent—allowing you to follow your passions, whims, curiosities, and stifled sense of adventure.

That's what this book is all about, as well as Hung and I's Digital Freedom Academy. It's a place where we hope to provide all of the educational tools and resources to make your escape from the bonds of employment a clean getaway. This book is to kick things off. I hope it inspires you to take action and change the course of your future. A freer and more fulfilling existence awaits…

ABOUT DIGITAL FREEDOM

So what exactly is "digital freedom?"

The word "digital" is probably not perfectly accurate, but the phrase "digital nomad" has sprung up in recent years to describe someone who makes a living online, and uses that location-untetheredness to travel the world—hitting up places like Chang Mai, Thailand, various islands, and other neat places filled with cheap ethnic food and young adventurers from all over the world.

But the "nomad" thing is just too limiting. I don't like it. You don't have to be a chic world traveler to enjoy the spoils of digital freedoms. I'm a little sick of traveling to be honest, and I probably wouldn't be doing much of it if it weren't for my girlfriend and her daughter. I'm using my freedom to help THEM see the world and do adventurous stuff that they didn't have the opportunity to do before I came along.

Also, having digital freedom doesn't mean that goofing off will deliver some kind of utopian existence. Traveling, doing adventurous things, recreating outdoors, and just generally having fun don't deliver enough true fulfillment to satisfy many human beings. Fun can only take us so far. We desperately need to feel important, to accomplish things, to be challenged, and to grow. All of those things create a sense of *progress*, which I consider to be one of the great keys to human happiness.

For no matter how many attractive people you fornicate with, no matter how many gnarly waves you surf, and no matter how many countries you visit or diamonds you buy—stagnation can still set in. And stagnation is an awful place to be. Happiness only exists when there is progress taking place. If you aren't making any progress in life and are totally happy, you most likely have a brain tumor or you're high right now.

With progress comes a greater sense of fulfillment—that feeling of satisfaction that no video game high score could ever really yield. It comes from having done meaningful work. It comes from doing something that is difficult, not easy. It comes from going beyond your normal capabilities to do something that is, by your standards, exceptional.

At 28, when my "vacation your way to happiness" mind-set was at its peak, I came across a really level-headed guy that snapped me out of this naive trance I'd been in since high school. At the time I was starting to get pretty damn depressed even though I was living a 3-minute walk from Kamaole beach in Maui, experiencing the best health of my life, and living an almost completely stress-free life.

I thought, because I wasn't happy when I should clearly be, that I needed to meditate or something. I read Eckhart Tolle daily and was always trying to snap into "the now" haha.

Thankfully, before I drifted too far into La La Land, Dr. John DeMartini whipped my delusional ass into shape real quick.

One of his far-too-many cute little sayings was, "Short-term fun equals long-term pain."

And sure enough, after a decade of trying to "fun" my way to happiness, I wasn't that happy of a camper at all. I needed to fucking DO something. I needed to accomplish something. I needed to challenge myself. I needed to get out of my comfort zone. I needed to fulfill at least some of the potential I had in me that was stagnating away on the beach.

After months of reflection I realized that my life was clearly governed by my interest in health and nutrition. It was funny, as without DeMartini's help, I really don't know if I would have even realized it. I was like a fish in water not realizing it was in water, or however that cliché goes.

But with this reflection I realized that it was what I thought about the most, it was the primary reason I moved to Maui in the first place (my asthma was better there), most of my expendable income was spent on expensive, organic foods that I bought mostly for health reasons (or juicers, supplements, exercise equipment, yoga classes, and so on), I read health books faster than books on any other subject and remembered the details better, it was what I steered conversations towards when in mixed company, and the list goes on and on.

So, instead of just passively living my life dedicated to health and nutrition, I decided to actively pursue the subject. I ordered 25 books or so (more than I had read in my life up to that point), and set out to read all of them in a year (I had always failed at achieving goals, so I was pretty convinced this would fizzle out and be something to feel miserable about after, per the usual outcome).

But, when aligning my goals with who I really was and what I really cared about, the outcome was quite different. I read all of those books in just half a year, read another 25 later that year, and went on to read over 300. I read thousands of studies, hundreds of websites, and absolutely lived and breathed the subject for seven solid years—meanwhile writing 800 or so articles, answering 6,000 comments on my site, filming over 100 videos, recording dozens of hours of audio, giving hundreds of hours of consultations both free and paid, and publishing 15 books (many of which are now unpublished due to being out-of-date with my current beliefs). In the process I became a bit of a mini-celebrity in the alternative health and nutrition scene online.

Best of all, I became smarter, more educated, more eloquent, and more confident in the process. And I managed to make more money than I ever had in my life and permanently exited the workforce while I was at it.

And you know what? Accomplishing all of that was a hell of a lot better than snorkeling with sea turtles in Maui, trekking in Nepal, reeling in huge salmon every day before work at a fishing lodge in Alaska, and every other recreational type of activity that I pursued in the ten years of adulthood preceding my intense "independent health and nutrition investigation."

So yeah, screw the whole "digital nomad" thing. You can do that if you want, but there are more types of freedom that the digital world can provide than the ability to travel. I travelled plenty before I even owned a computer with an internet connection. The freedom I have now—the freedom to create, to take any idea and turn it into a viable business in a matter of just a couple months, to reach tens of thousands of people with my thoughts and ideas on any given day, to help touch the lives of others in a meaningful way, to create earning opportunities for over a dozen others all over the world (my extended team), and to show my family a life of adventure...

Those are the digital freedoms I personally enjoy the most these days (although I certainly have no regrets about all the great adventures of my 20's when attempting the whole permavacation thing). And you can go out there and enjoy whatever freedoms inspire you most at this current point in your life. That might be taking a few years off just to ski and play golf. It may be using your freedom to make a huge impact in the world with your innovative ideas. Who knows. That's up for you to decide, and I hope I can help facilitate the freedom you seek.

To digital freedom!

WHY YOU MUST START EARNING INTERNET-BASED INCOME

Whether you are old, young, rich, poor, smart, stupid, wanting to travel, hate travel, love your job, hate your job, are good with computers, or are totally techtarded (like me), you should really give earning internet-based income a shot. It can be with the intent of being a full-time thing or the trendy-phrased "side hustle." But you should consider learning how to make money on the internet a mandatory part of your education, at any age. It's like math, only a lot more important, a lot more useful, and a lot easier. Screw math.

Okay, I actually like math, and I'm fairly good at it, and it is important, but I just wanted to sound cool.

Like any science or art, learning how to do it (make money online) yields an ever-increasing hunger to learn more. And, as you learn more and get more practice, it keeps getting easier and making more and more intuitive sense.

Do yourself a favor. Follow Hung's advice and START. The biggest hurdle to being successful with any endeavor online or off is failure to start.

The second biggest hurdle to overcome is failure to continue. I was a rare case in that I was so inspired and passionate about what I was doing in health and nutrition that I was going to keep doing it whether I made money at it or not.

And because of that, I made it through two years of making no money at all followed by a year of making only around $6,000. Year four still couldn't pay all my bills. It wasn't until year five that I finally made $40,000 and was making more than I was spending. Five years!

That lengthy (and totally unnecessary if I had known what I was doing) time to reach success inspired the creation of an entire alter persona (Buck Flogging), six short books, and a course and website called *Quit Your Job in 6 Months* (QuitN6 for short: www.QuitN6.com).

But if you can start AND continue, you'll reach success. Armed with the fruits of my experience, I hope to help make that first hurdle much smaller and help you get over the second hurdle much faster.

I still haven't really answered the question of why you absolutely must start earning income online though. The answer to that question lies in a very fast-changing world. Automation, robotics, and the sheer speed of technology in general makes no job safe. One day you're working at Blockbuster video and the next day Netflix pops up and you're out of a job.

We all can grasp that example, but that sort of shift is occurring in just about every industry, and those shifts are happening more abruptly and more violently as technology continues to advance at an accelerated pace.

Global economics continue to grow more and more unstable as well. It's a time of great upheaval the world over. Capitalism itself will likely become obsolete for such a dynamic world in just a few decades. Citizens of the world will no longer tolerate dramatic booms, busts, and bubbles that hit real people's finances like natural disasters.

And you can bet that such a transition will be one filled with turmoil and instability so great it would be hard for us to grasp from our current point of view.

I think the only way to keep up and achieve any kind of stability is not to rely on the old 9 to 5 in a time when businesses, entire industries, and even whole COUNTRIES are collapsing, but to learn the skills of earning internet-based money. The speed of the internet is amazing. Digital Freedom Academy itself went from idea to live website collecting money in under two weeks. Most of my books and sites all went from conception to generating revenue in under two months.

In a world moving at the speed of lightning, having the power to quickly pivot, seize opportunities in a flash, and make ideas into a source of sustenance for you and your loved ones is the greatest form of economic security. Even if all of my current websites collapsed tomorrow, I wouldn't be the least bit concerned. With the skills, knowledge, experience, and relationships I have built, I could be back to earning a full-time living for myself in a month or two, if not in a matter of weeks.

Financial security, although it's undeniably important, is not very uplifting or exciting though. There are lots of other reasons why you should push yourself beyond your comfort zone and start navigating your way through the world of internet business.

One that I've brought up already is the power to turn your ideas into living, breathing entities earning money in a very short amount of time. I mentioned the beauty of this when it comes to having some financial security in an unstable world, but in this case I'm talking just the pure joy and excitement of it.

Having the power to allow your ideas to materialize is one of the greatest powers you'll ever know. I can't say enough about how invigorating it is. It's so invigorating that it's easy to get overworked. I personally have had to step away from being so glued into my websites, because it was so exciting that I was ignoring my physical needs. Turns out humans aren't supposed to stare at a glowing monitor, motionless in a chair for over 12 hours a day. Who knew?!! ☺

This brings up another reason why you should dive head first into the digital earning universe: working on your own shit is fun.

You always hear stories of how people start a business and end up working themselves into oblivion—their businesses completely taking over their lives. This isn't just because starting a business requires a lot of work. It's because working on your own business, where the sky is the limit in terms of how well it could do if things fall into place just perfectly, is addictive. It's extremely exciting, and it feels a lot more like playing video games or watching YouTube videos and having trouble turning off the monitor. It's hard to eat, sleep, or do anything but think about your project or projects at times. It's not like "work" at all.

I'm not saying all work is bad or can't be fun, but working on your own enterprise is truly the spice of life. Having the freedom to actually do that with the power of the internet—with virtually no need for startup money, investments, or other barriers or complications—is indescribably great.

Along the same lines, the digital world is an endless world of possibilities, and you have opportunities to do exactly what you find most interesting and actually make money pursuing it, in ways that no job could ever really provide. And while there is a ton of lip service being paid by countless cheesedicks on how we should all be trying to "follow our passion" in life, I must agree that a life lived in pursuit of passion is without question more fulfilling than one that isn't.

How we spend our time is probably THE most important thing in life. Never before in human history have people been able to create paid opportunities to explore their curiosities, dreams, hobbies, and interests to the extent we can now. And those who don't seize this great gold rush of opportunity to replace mundaneness with exhilaration are really missing out.

While it may feel hazy how you can turn a personal interest into something that pays the bills, hopefully the lengthy discussion in Part III of this book will give you some idea of how others have—and how you—can indeed create financial opportunity online out of just about any hobby, curiosity, interest, or idea.

And that's why you should absolutely get into the digital game as soon as you can. If you really want your life to change for the better, you must figure out what you like, how you like spending your time, and figure out how to get paid to do that. The internet has the answer to that last question.

A great life is one where you get to spend almost all of your time doing something you love to do, but the best life is one where you get paid to do that. With the endless abyss of opportunities that the digital world has opened up in the last two decades, achieving that isn't woefully improbable anymore. You really SHOULD try to achieve that, and you shouldn't stop trying until you've succeeded.

Part III
HOW MONEY IS MADE ONLINE

By Matt Stone

INTRODUCTION

Geez, that's enough of a Tony Robbins-esque pep-talk. Sheesh. I was making myself sick with all that hyperbole. Time to dig into some meat and potatoes and discuss how money is made online. I think once you get a full overview of how it all goes down, and how people are succeeding with a wide spectrum of things, you'll stop feeling like you're not special enough to do it, too. Just about anyone can do it, you just have to dive in and overcome your insecurities.

And believe me, I get the insecurity thing. I've always been a confident person (okay, cocky dickhead really). But when it came to earning money online, I really had trouble believing that I could *actually* do it. One thing happened that really changed that for me though.

I was making about $1,200 per month from the sale of a few books I had written. Those books were bought by followers of my blog, YouTube channel, and social media pages mostly. I had some pretty impressive traffic, lots of loyalty from my fanbase as evidenced by the hundreds of comments left on nearly every blog post I wrote, and was doing well in every category except dollars.

But then I began publicizing the work of someone else. He was a health practitioner doing some things that I was interested in, so I went to visit him, documented some of the things he was doing, and created a great deal of excitement amongst my fans. In a matter of weeks, I watched him sell somewhere in the neighborhood of $60,000 worth of products—all from just a handful of blog posts I had written!

Here I was earning peanuts, but I saw the true earning potential that I had failed to recognize before. Boom. Immediately my mind travelled to a higher tier where I not only believed but *expected* to start making considerably more money—whereas before I was actually pretty pleased that I was making anything at all.

A month or so later I published a couple of books documenting my experiences with this health practitioner and pocketed $12,000 in about a week. I've never made anywhere near a measly $1,200 in a month since.

So how can you make that same shift? Simple. It's called the Law of Attraction. You just think happy thoughts all day and then your Paypal account starts blowing up like you hit the jackpot on a slot machine.

Totally fucking kidding. When someone mentions the supposed Law of Attraction (that like attracts like supposedly, which is totally backwards—see magnetism), I'm less likely to be their friend had they mentioned stockpiling dead bodies in their crawl space.

The real answer? Well shit, I don't know. I had to have that personal experience, and when I did, my entirely self-fabricated limitations were lifted like a switch had been flipped. So know that your self-doubts about your ability to succeed are probably entirely false. Jump on one foot while listening to Tony Robbins motivational speeches backwards and you too will have that switch flipped. All paths eventually lead back to Tony.

Seriously though. Work on it. Almost everyone that I see fail or stay stuck in that $500-$1,000 per month no man's land are stuck in a weird, pussy-footed vortex of sorts. Drives me nuts. I just want to give them a *Moonstruck* Cher-slap. "Snap out of it!"

Okay, well that was kind of a weird tirade, but it wouldn't be a Matt Stone book without at least a few nonsensical tangents and too many movie references.

Now let's ACTUALLY dig into those aforementioned meat and potatoes as promised. How do people make money online? This may be basic stuff for some of you, but the discussion should provide some value to you know-it-alls. Those of you who are completely clueless about how money is made online are in for an eye-opener...

BLOGGING

"I'm not even sure what a blog is."

That was my favorite thing that people said when I mentioned making a living as a blogger and author.

It was usually stated with both confusion and a little bit of snootiness like I was just part of some weird techno-fad that was soon to fizzle out and leave me penniless while all the khakied frat boys with Master's Degrees living in the suburbs with two kids were winning the game of life with their "smart career choices."

Now I frequently send out email broadcasts that bring in as much as $10,000, and I don't even write them. Take that you snooty "don't know what a blog is" jerkface poo-poo heads! Have fun reading your newspapers and trying to get your scratched CD's to play without skipping.

Yes, I made money as a blogger. But I didn't do a very good job at making money blogging. I took the high and mighty road and only made money with the sale of my books, audio, and video. I didn't do any of that affiliate stuff, refused to advertise on my site, turned up my nose at the network marketing opportunities that have made most of my old blogger friends rich by now, and refused to commercially taint my site and brand in any way.

Because I didn't make money blogging in the traditional ways, which we'll discuss in a sec, I really developed a disdain for blogging. I always wanted to be a respected author, and I only wanted to be compensated for the sale of those books and related educational materials. Because of that, I saw the folly in publishing hundreds and hundreds of blog posts when I could have been publishing more books and other products for sale and actually making money.

And so I "killed my blog"—focusing instead on getting email subscribers at the exclusion of everything else—and developed the previously-mentioned anti-blogging character Buck Flogging (as in Fuck Blogging).

But in all honesty, my firm stance against blogging is a little overstated. Blogging is a unique form of communication, and it's fun as hell. It can also be extremely lucrative if you embrace blogging for what it is and seize all of the great money-earning opportunities with it.

So how do people make money blogging? There are three primary ways of earning income with a blog, and plenty more secondary ways of earning income.

Primary Blogging Income Sources:

1. **Advertising** — A blog is a great way to generate A LOT of traffic and pageviews to a site. But this traffic isn't there to shop, they are there to check out some short, insightful, controversial, entertaining, or otherwise interesting short piece of free content. While they may not be there to shop, advertisers want to be in front of people wherever they congregate. Advertisers that sell products that your specific followership might like are always eager to pay to show up on your site in places such as your sidebar, below the header, or even interspersed in your blog content itself. Advertisers typically pay per pageview. It's not much. Maybe just a penny per pageview, but if you have heavy traffic, it can add up. You can also install something

like Google Adwords on your site, and they will try to match their users' ads to your content, paying you per click that your blog generates on their ads. Again, this is not a huge moneymaker per click, but it can add up if you manage to draw in a lot of traffic. Traffic is money. If you can get people reading what you write, it has value, and you can make a living doing it.

2. **Sponsorship** — Sponsorship is pretty rare, but if your content is really well-matched to a specific industry or niche, you might be able to attract a full-on sponsor. It's basically just an advertiser that wants exclusive advertising rights to the people who congregate on your site, and they are willing to pay a premium for it. It's also a nice, regular paycheck, which is quite a luxury in the digital world.

3. **Affiliate Income** — Affiliate income is similar to advertising income, but there are many more opportunities to earn, and the earnings are often much greater. For example, you could write a big feature article on a fitness blog about the latest Fitbit model. By using an affiliate link and linking to the product, everyone who finds that article, clicks on your link, and ends up buying a Fitbit online will give you credit for that sale, and you'll earn a percentage of the sale amount. Affiliate selling is its own universe, and it's fun and interesting. I'll discuss it in depth later on in the book. But to be sure, the highest-paid bloggers typically take advantage of affiliate-selling opportunities in hundreds of innovative ways.

If you are just a straight blogger, and you have nothing for sale—you just write blog posts—you'll earn most if not all of your income from those sources. But the most successful bloggers create other opportunities for themselves once they've garnered a following. Lots of traffic and a big, loyal readership is a powerful thing. I've always considered fans to be money in the bank. I can "go to the ATM" anytime by writing a new book, creating a course, offering coaching or consultations, or even launching entire new websites and businesses, which I have done many times (too many times, haha!).

Those topics will again be featured in more depth later in the book. Suffice it to say that blogging is a viable way to earn a living online, it can be really fun, I absolutely loved it, my success was built on the foundation I built blogging, and I owe a lot to it—and probably shouldn't bash it so much.

The reason I do bash it is because I see so many people who don't really want to be blogging trying to blog to garner a following because they've been told they have to blog (or that blogging is a great way to build a readership interested in their books and other digital products), and all of that is nonsense. Blogging is a slow and laborious way to garner a following, you don't need to blog at all to get people interested in your books, courses, coaching, or services. And having a blog with tons of content and a shitload of traffic doesn't mean you'll sell your products and services. I can't tell you how many massive blogging successes I've come across that can't sell a $3 book of theirs to save their lives. It doesn't always translate.

If you want to blog, you should blog your little fingers down to nubs and have fun with it. But if you don't, please don't feel obligated to. Most aren't very good at blogging (it is a skill and an art unto itself), and most who blog never get any kind of loyal following built. Even if they start getting a ton of traffic from Google searches, they often still don't sell their products and services very well. How blogging became viewed as both a necessary and effective marketing tactic for selling products and services drives me nuts. That's what I'm revolting against with my whole "Buck Flogging" shenanigans.

Of course you've heard of blogging, you know people can make money doing it, and you probably know someone who earns at least a little money from a blog. No grand revelations there. You probably want to get some insider secret on how to be a successful blogger, and I will indulge that, because, as they say, "Buck never disappoints."

So how do you become a successful blogger? I've thought about it at great length for a decade now, and I think the keys to successful blogging are the following 5 things:

1. **Pick subject matter that a large percentage of the general public finds interesting.** The most popular subject matter includes things like celebrity gossip, politics, news, health and fitness, cooking, making money, controversial views and conspiracy, and humor—stuff that makes its way into the checkout aisle at the supermarket. You can be successful in smaller niches for sure, but your primary blogging revenue sources will be lower because your total traffic is likely to be much lower.

2. **Be engaging, outspoken, entertaining, irreverent, polarizing, controversial, or otherwise bold in your writing.** Being a successful blogger is all about impact, and making an impact comes from being very bold in some way. A blog is a great place to let your opinions, emotions, and sense of humor flourish. You should be who you are in private, which is likely an opinionated, crass, funny, outspoken person—not the polite and subdued person you are when you're in the company of strangers or new acquaintances. Blogging is about having a personality bigger than life. You should turn up the volume on

your personality and go big. If people are fighting in the comments section, you're doing something right!

3. **Spend more time marketing yourself and your blog on social media and other blogs than you do posting new articles.** This is pretty self-explanatory, but most just want to write little articles and wait for the world to discover them. Passionately and obsessively sharing your content in as many places as possible is a much speedier way to build an audience and a lot of traffic. Refuse to let your blog posts go unread!

4. **Network with other bloggers and influencers in your niche.** Bloggers just want exposure, and getting to know other bloggers in your niche can open up a lot of guest-posting opportunities and much more. Don't be a little digital hermit unless you are really going to war against the perspectives and beliefs of other bloggers in your niche, in which case don't pull any punches (this can also be an effective way to leverage the audiences built by other bloggers, as they won't be able to resist blogging about how wrong they think you are!). One way or another, make sure you know the bloggers in your niche, and make sure they know who you are as well.

5. **Be relentless, or at least consistent.** Posting erratically or infrequently can kill a blogger's audience-gathering momentum in short order. Post at least once per week, and if you do post that infrequently, that blog post better be really polished and powerful. Otherwise post something several times per week, every day, or even multiple times per day. You do that consistently for a while, focusing on content with broad appeal, in bold fashion, dedicated to sharing your content wherever you can and getting to know the other bloggers in your space, and you'll definitely get somewhere with it.

Of course, all of the tips above are predicated on the idea that your site is optimized for turning the traffic you attract into dollars and cents from advertisers, affiliate programs, and other opportunities that you take advantage of along the way, such as launching your own books, courses, coaching, etc. Don't ignore the economic and analytical side of things because you are "not into that kind of thing," "don't care about money," or "an artist." You're not. You're just being a dumbass and avoiding learning something new because doing so is uncomfortable and not very fun. You know what else isn't fun? Going back to work at the job you did at age 19 because your blog didn't make enough money, having to move in with your mom, or having your girlfriend dump you because she thinks you're a loser (all three of these things actually happened to me, because I refused to go out of my comfort zone and took way too long to reach success).

Okay, let's move on from blah blah blogging (yuck!) and onto bigger and better things!

NETWORK MARKETING

It's funny that I just used the word "yuck" to end the last chapter, as I think that's what most people think when they encounter network marketing—also known as direct marketing, multilevel marketing, and that goddamn pyramid scheme shit.

Like I said earlier though, most of my old, shameless blogger pals from the good old days have gone on to embrace network marketing, and most of the ones who have are now pretty rich. I'm talking about spouses-quitting-their-jobs kind of money.

It wasn't easy—they absolutely worked their asses off—but several DOZEN of them are making $10,000 per month or more after a couple years of focused effort. They are all making more money than they did from blogging.

While network marketing has a bad reputation (I published a short book about it once, and people started treating me like a registered sex offender at a Chuck E. Cheese), you can't deny that it's a viable way to achieve employer-free financial freedom. We all know someone who has done well with it. But most of the success stories we've heard of are by those obnoxious, overzealous, social butterfly types who put together those cringeworthy "parties" and other shenanigans. Gross. I'd rather just have a job than toss all of my self-respect into the trashcan like that. Hey though, if you're into it, give 'em hell. Whatever floats your boat.

But my compadres in the health and nutrition blogger world pulled it all off without doing any of that—they did it in true digital fashion over phone and internet from the comfort of their own homes. And these homes smell of cinnamon and lavender, cuz they all did it with essential oils.

That's right. Those little nice-scented bottles of plant extracts known as essential oils are all paying their bills and then some.

I personally have always liked essential oils, probably because I've been on the crunchy hippie side since my late teens. I once even wore wooden jewelry and, as I've already painfully admitted, read Eckhart Tolle. I'm not proud of it, but I also can't deny it.

These days I don't really do any new agey things other than having mediocre personal hygiene. But my house still smells of clove and frankincense. My girlfriend got all peanut butter and jealous of my blogger pals and is now well on her way to becoming the next essential oil tycoon, so our place is overrun with little bottles of nice-smelling things.

The nice thing about the successful digital network marketers I know is that they haven't needed an army of tens of thousands to make it work. Just by lining up a half dozen to a dozen attendees on frequent webinars is usually enough to add new recruits, and because the methods they use to be successful are more easily replicable than the whole "annoy all your friends and family, attack strangers, and throw a bunch of cheesy parties" method, the recruits they bring in have a high success rate.

Okay, the "party" method certainly works, too. I really shouldn't bash it. It's just that anything involving actually having to interact with humans in person is just SOOOO 1979. I mean seriously, who actually hangs out with real people in person anymore? Okay, I have social problems, haha. Damn digital freedom.

There's no doubt that in network marketing, the key is not selling a ton of product or even recruiting a ton of people to be distributors. The key is being able to help the people you recruit become successful themselves. In network marketing lingo, this is called "successful duplication." If what you do can be duplicated, then the people in your downline will be successful, and if the people in your downline are successful, you too will be successful.

The digital era, from what I've witnessed, has made being successful in network marketing A LOT easier. You might put your biases against network marketing aside and recon-sider it—especially if you have a burning desire to be digitally free, but you don't have any special skills or expertise allow-ing you to become a hot shot author, blogger, freelancer, or expert of some kind.

Enough of that talk. Let's move on to some other excit-ing stuff. If selling essential oils is something you're curious about, feel free to reach out to my girlfriend Andie at: ezentialoils.com

EMAIL MARKETING

Now we're talking! I loved blogging, and I've made plenty of money selling books I've written and the like, but I've become a huge fan of email marketing over the last three years. In this chapter we'll talk about how many of my sites make money, which includes thorough discussion on making money as an affiliate, how I've built some big email lists, and more.

Since I paid to have my very first website designed, which went live on January 1 of 2009, I've known that capturing email addresses and building a "list" as it's commonly referred to, is a powerful thing. Everyone in the know shouts this from the rooftops, and it intuitively makes sense. Being able to send out an email broadcast and have your words, videos, and more land right in the email inbox of all of your followers, is a powerful thing. You can communicate with people on your terms rather than simply hope that they remember to check your site or pay attention to you on social media.

But no one really shows you how. I mean sure. In my blogging era I put a little free offer in the sidebar to get some free information in exchange for an email address, but that never worked. Even when I was getting 5,000 website visits daily I was still only getting 10 new subscribers per day. It makes sense. How often do you just hand over your email address because there is a little box off to the side on some-one's website? I don't know if I've ever done it.

But one day, a half decade into my internet business pursuits, I took the time to Google "how to build an email list." It didn't take long before I found a video on YouTube where a guy demonstrated how to build a "lead page." I'd never heard of such a concept.

During the video, where he built a page with a few sentences and an optin box laid over an image of a sports car, he mentioned how around 50% of the people visiting his lead pages were subscribing.

I stopped the video. I thought I misheard him and rewound it a few seconds.

Sure enough, he said 50%. 50%!

That means that if 1,000 people visit his page, 500 would make their way onto his email list. I was floored. I had no idea such a thing was possible. While I didn't make any immediate changes, I filed this idea away right in the front row, and it bothered me for quite some time until I finally decided to do something about it. The whole story is a story indeed—one I turned into an entire book you can read called, *Kill Your Blog*.

The short version of the story is that I became obsessed with building an email list at all costs. I now create these mysteri-ous "lead pages," where visitors to it have nothing else to do but either subscribe to my mailing list or leave the page, with a 50%+ conversion rate quite routinely. In 34 months of ded-icated list building, I've gathered a few hundred thousand email addresses. With blogging I only managed to build a list of a few thousand, even with many millions of visits to my site. And it's changed absolutely *everything* for me. It feels like money grows on trees.

Before I go into detail about how I make money by sending out emails, let me first tell you how I get traffic to my lead pages (or what I usually refer to as "optin pages") in more detail. I don't want you left feeling like I've been vague or that I'm hiding something so that I can swindle you into buying something later. I'm not.

But keep in mind that this book is primarily intended to provide an introductory education about how money is made online, while painting a general picture of how it's accomplished. Really showing you everything requires a lot of audio and video, and is beyond the scope of a mere book. Hopefully I can give you a good idea though, and make it seem doable. It absolutely is. In fact, the way I build an audience is much easier than what most people are doing (blogging, podcasting, trying to stir up buzz on social media, etc.).

I get traffic to my optin pages by leveraging the audiences that others have already built. Instead of going out and blogging or podcasting my brains out for multiple years to build some traction, trying to connect with followers one-by-one, I expedite the whole process by reaching out to those who have already put in all the hard work, and getting them to drive as much traffic to my optin pages as possible.

How do I get them to do this? My incredible charm and good looks of course!

No, I get them to send subscribers my way by doing two very simple things:

1. **Creating an awesome, free event and inviting them to participate.** This works because everyone loves to tell

their audience about something that's free and awesome. If it's free and awesome, that means the value is off the charts. Telling your audience about something that's really great that they will love that costs them absolutely nothing builds goodwill and trust with your audience. It's great for everyone involved. Participants also get great exposure for their work, as there are usually dozens of participants all sending traffic to the event. My "events" (and I'm the only one to do this that I'm aware of) are large bundles of free books and courses that participants are willing to share. I run these events for 11 days and average 45,000 new subscribers per event. That's not a typo.

2. **Paying them per lead.** That's right, not only do you give them something their audience will love that gives them free exposure to prospective fans and customers, you pay them, too! While it's not a ton of money, it's guaranteed and doesn't require pushing something for sale. It's pretty irresistible. I typically pay $1-2 per lead depending on the event and the site it's for. That may sound scary, and you may be thinking, "I don't have any money, so I couldn't do that." However, I get the leads, make money, and *then* pay them—usually three months after the event. While this is a little risky until you know how much money a typical subscriber is worth, you can start out paying them as little as 25 cents and still get some participation—and more subscribers than I got in seven years of blogging.

To be sure, there is no better way to get email subscribers that I'm aware of. Every overnight list-building success I've ever witnessed relied upon creating something cool that people could get for free by entering their email address, and finding a way to pay people for referring traffic to that optin page—either by paying them per lead (like I do), or selling something within a few weeks of subscribing and giving the referring affiliate a portion of the sale amount (usually 50% or higher). The latter is safer and more common, but affiliates usually don't get paid much or promote as eagerly when there is no guaranteed commission.

One site, www.thetruthaboutcancer.com, managed to draw over a million subscribers in just a few weeks with a similar approach. It works. And it's a great way to create tons of mutually beneficial relationships with the leaders in your industry.

Getting subscribers doesn't mean much if you don't know how to keep them and get them to spend money. I don't mean to sound like one of those "business" people by focusing on the money component, but at the end of the day it matters a lot. Your ability to get subscribers, grow into something big and impactful, and reach people with the value you and your business have to offer depends on your ability to make money. Money is a fantastic tool to reach people. I love making it, and not because I throw it all into my bank account and giggle ominously. Making money allows me to hire people—creating awesome opportunities for people who love to have digital freedom—and it allows me to pay the affiliates who send me subscribers. I live for creating opportunities for people in my niche to earn money. It's more thrilling than making it for my own personal gain. For real.

So let's talk about making money from the subscribers you get.

I've benefitted tremendously from simplifying my internet business down to the amount of money it takes to get a subscriber and the amount of money I make from each subscriber. I call the amount of money I make "Revenue Per Subscriber (RPS)." In my experience, any site that makes

$5 per subscriber in 30 days or less from the start of that subscription can succeed with relative ease. Making less than that makes things difficult. It's hard to get a truly quality subscriber for less than a few dollars, and that $5 mark needs to be reached, and reached fairly quickly, to keep growing the business from being a struggle.

Later in the book we'll talk at length about selling products that you create yourself, such as courses, subscriptions, services, and more. For now, let's take this opportunity to talk about making money selling other people's products and services as an affiliate. I don't recommend trying to ONLY sell other people's products and services with the email list you build, mostly because you'll likely have to wait 2-3 months to get paid, and this means the amount of time it takes you to make a decent amount of revenue per subscriber is delayed. This delay can cause cashflow problems, limit your ability to run advertising campaigns, and otherwise make your life suck.

But I have several websites that rely almost exclusively on affiliate income, and, while they aren't ideal businesses—mostly because I really underestimated the crippling effect of having to wait to receive payment from various affiliate programs when I started them—they make some good money and are successful enterprises to be sure.

In real life, when I try to explain how making money as an affiliate works, I notice people tend to instantly tune out as if I'm describing something impossibly complicated that they have no chance of grasping. I'm not sure why it's so scary to people. It's very simple really.

We all know how Wal-Mart's business works. They don't make many of the products for sale on their shelves. They sell other people's products and keep half of the proceeds from the sale. Because they don't have to make it all themselves, they can provide a nearly infinite selection of cheap, shitty products for hillbillies to shop for in the comfort of their own pajamas.

The internet has far more products and services available for sale than what Wal-Mart could ever possibly carry on their shelves, and you can play the role of Wal-Mart—making as much or more per unit sold than the person who created the product or service. It's a remarkably easy way to make a living, and email marketing is the most efficient way to do it.

Take for example the most successful affiliate promotion I've ever done—Chandler Bolt and James Roper's *Self-Publishing School.*

Chandler and James run a great business that pulls in over a million bucks a year helping people fulfill their dreams of becoming authors. They are great guides and motivators—making sure that all of their students follow through and actually get a professional product up for sale on Amazon.

Each student, depending on which package they buy, might spend anywhere from $600-$3,000 for Self-Publishing School. As an affiliate, I get 40% of any sales from customers that I send over to their site. This is all tracked automatically with affiliate tracking software. My link is unique to me. And what's really cool is that I can use an affiliate link to send people over to get a free video series. If it leads to a sale days or even weeks later, I still get credit.

With bonuses, I've made upwards of $30,000 during a launch of just a few weeks.

Self-Publishing School is just one example. With lots of different lists and lots of different websites, I've made more than $10,000 promoting Thrive Market, a bodyweight exercise bundle, a big bundle of books through Ultimate Bundles, and a handful of other really big promotions.

With Amazon, who offers up to 8.5% on all of the products a person purchases within 24 hours of clicking on an affiliate link of mine, I've made over $200,000! I made most of that through Buck Books, where I send people over to Amazon to check out free and 99-cent books. If they buy one of these books, I make a mere 8.5 cents. It's not much. But if they buy $100 worth of other books, groceries, back-to-school supplies, laundry detergent and kitty litter while they are there (or even the next day before the 24-hour cookie expires), I get $8.50 for being the person that sent them over there to shop.

Now you know how Amazon got so many customers! They have hundreds of thousands of people like me sending them traffic and earning some great money doing it.

Note, don't get TOO excited about Amazon's affiliate program when it comes to email marketing. Unfortunately, it's against their terms and conditions to put affiliate links in emails. They aren't trying to be meanies. In fact, they want your affiliate links in emails. My impression is that this can only be done if your email marketing service is hosted in one of eight approved states (I don't know which eight states, and they don't disclose that information). They contacted me personally, and fortunately, I lucked out. Not only did they give me special permission to do so, they encouraged me to do so. All I can say to you is that if you're thinking about trying it, you do so at your own risk!

But don't worry. There are a ton of other affiliate offers and affiliate platforms you can take advantage of...

Clickbank has tens of thousands of products you can promote and earn a commission on (usually 75%), and Clickbank is just one of dozens of major affiliate networks with thousands of products to choose from.

It's pointless to try to list all of the affiliate opportunities, as just about everything for sale on the internet pays people to send customers their way via an affiliate program. Your task is to find the best services and products that match up to the interests and desires of the email list you've built. Then, as tastefully and tactfully as you can, let your subscribers know about these great services and products, leaving your affiliate link in the email broadcasts you send out to them.

It may sound too good to be true, but it really can be this simple.

Again, you didn't get this book to find out that you can make money as an affiliate for all kinds of products. You probably already knew that. You want to know the real secrets to being successful. I hope to go into much greater detail in a separate book or course someday, but for now, I think I can summarize the secrets to successful email marketing into a few simple steps:

1. **In your writing, be shockingly honest, authentic, vulnerable, funny, or otherwise interesting and engaging.** Just like with blogging, you can't be a dud. You have to find a way to make your personality larger and louder so that you can be memorable, entice people to actually open and read your emails carefully, and ultimately connect. Don't be too vanilla. It's better to make a strong connection with 20% of the people that subscribe while 80% hate you than to try to please everyone and make a weak connection with 100% of your subscribers.

2. **Email your list frequently—at least a couple times per week.** While many people are afraid to email their list frequently, probably because every time they send an email

to their list they inevitably have some people unsubscribe, I think this is a mistake. We're all competing for people's attention, and you do that best with frequent reminders of your existence. Sure, some people will feel like you are bombarding them with too many emails and unsubscribe, but you'll make the people who like hearing from you often very happy. That matters more. Emailing frequently also gives you more opportunities to share content, provide value to your peeps, and promote various offers that you believe in. Get them used to paying attention and hearing from you often.

3. **Get to know your stats**. A certain percentage of people will open your emails. Some will click on the links you are promoting and some will not. Of the ones that click through to the offer you are promoting, some will buy and some won't. Some will spend a lot of money and some will spend a little. You should know these stats, pay attention to these stats, and use these stats to choose better promotions and learn what your audience does and doesn't like. You should watch to see what headlines get the highest rate of email opens from your list. You should know how many people unsubscribe every time you send out a broadcast, so you can learn what they like and what seems to turn them off. Ultimately, at the end of the day, the stats that matter most when trying to figure out what to promote to your audience are the number of clicks you send over and the amount of money you earn per click (called "earnings per click," or "EPC").

4. **Learn how to resend to unopens and do it often.** Most email service providers like Aweber, Active Campaign, Ontraport, and others give you the ability to create separate lists of who opened your email and who didn't. Usually 60-70%+ of your subscribers will not even open

your email. Those bastards! Instead of resending the email to your entire list, risking annoying the ones who saw it the first time, resend your email to unopens for a couple rounds. Instead of 30% of people opening your email, you'll be able to get more than 50% of your list to open your email. I don't do this for every email, but if I promote something that performs well and makes a lot of money (the email gets a lot of clicks and the EPC is higher than $1), I will resend to unopens multiple times and sometimes DOUBLE my earnings on a promotion because of it—all without bombarding the very best subscribers I have (the ones who were paying attention the first time I sent it out!).

5. **Don't be afraid to sell, but don't be too pushy or too salesy either.** It's bad to just sell, sell, sell all the time. We all know that (excluding sociopaths). I have some sites where I've managed to make it perfectly okay to make each email about things for sale because I have lists where people are subscribed to shop for discounted stuff, but if that's not what people signed up for, they'll be turned off quickly. However, if you go too long without mentioning anything for sale, you run the risk of entering sort of a "friend zone" type of vortex. Mix it up. Get them comfortable with hearing about some products and services for sale, but make sure they are excellent so that the ones who buy learn to trust your recommendations. How do you keep things from sounding too salesy? Just keep your authentic voice that you always communicate with, and insert something funny or radically honest. If you say a product is the best thing ever and has absolutely no flaws, people won't trust you. You'll sound like you're straight out of an infomercial, and everyone on your list with an IQ over 80 will quickly unsubscribe. If you show

radical honesty by pointing out the downsides, or you insert some humor to break things up and keep it from sounding like a sales pitch, you'll come off as being a lot more trustworthy. Trustworthiness is what will keep people on your list and buying stuff from you years down the road. It's very easy to achieve if you are 100% genuine, and you really do want to help people more than you want to help yourself. If you aren't, it's a really tough thing to fake. People have heard so many sales pitches in their lifetimes that they have a 6th sense for detecting bullshit. So you better be the real thing if you hope to have lasting success with email marketing (or any business).

Hopefully that gives you a good overview of email marketing. No matter what you hope to do online, building an email list will likely be the most powerful marketing tactic you find. I realize this chapter is hopelessly incomplete as a standalone guide on email marketing, but you can learn a ton more about it in book 3 of my completely FREE *Quit Your Job in 6 Months* series. You can grab that at: www.QuitN6.com/free-books

Next let's talk about what I'm doing right now—writing a book that will be self-published! I've sold over $500,000 of books that I've written every word of myself, I love it, and I know a ton about what it takes to be successful.

SELF-PUBLISHING

The first product I sold online was a dinky mess-of-a-pdf file that I called a "book" and slapped a $19.99 price tag on. This was January of 2009, not too long after Kindle was launched and when $39 eBooks were still widespread on the internet. The thing didn't even have a book cover! Just a brief description and a hideous Buy Now button. It's amazing I actually sold them, but I did. I sold almost 200 copies in my first year of trying to make money online in earnest.

That may not sound like a ton, but making $4,000 selling a sloppy 60-page pdf with no book cover probably puts that thing in the top 10% of all books written and sold. Yes, most books are epic catastrophes in the sales department. That's just reality. Kindle made it easier for authors to strike it rich for a while when it first launched, but it didn't take long for their platform to get flooded with eBooks for sale—making it extremely difficult to make good money publishing a book.

Yep. Sad news my friends. The good old days of publishing $39 eBooks and selling them like hotcakes, as well as the good old days of everyone with a keyboard and a pulse being able to publish on Amazon for instant cash, are already over. But opportunities still abound, books are still a great part of a well-rounded business, and writing is still what many consider to be the most freeing profession. I agree. It was trying to make my living with the written word that got me started with all this stuff in the first place.

Can you really make a living at it? Absolutely. If you're really driven to become a successful author, you can become one. In this chapter I'll do my best to share what I've learned—painting a realistic picture of what it's like to build a book-based online business.

Assuming you can write pretty well, and you like to write—and therefore could actually succeed at it given a chance—the first question you need to ask yourself is whether or not you'd like to publish your books on Amazon (and potentially other vendors as well, although it's hardly worth it), sell the books on your own site, sell your books through vendors like Clickbank, or a combination of more than one.

Most assume that publishing on Amazon is the way to go, but that's not necessarily the case. There are some huge advantages to selling your books on your own site or through other vendors, like Clickbank, especially for nonfiction authors, and especially ESPECIALLY if you have a combination of audio, video, and more that you can package or "bundle" with your book or books.

One advantage is that you can typically sell your books for more money when you sell them on your own site—well above $10, and upwards of $100 when bundled with a course or other valuable add-ons. When people are on your own site, they aren't comparison shopping at that point. If they are looking for a fat loss solution for example, you have a chance to sell them on your specific approach and trigger an impulse buy. They either buy or they don't. They don't buy someone else's book instead. You really aren't competing with anyone, just competing for the person's attention.

But you could never sell an eBook on Amazon for $20. With the way their ranking system works and the millions of other reading options at $9.99 and under—and especially with their Kindle Unlimited subscription that allows people to download as many books as they want for $9.99/month—a prospective buyer just isn't going to find your book description so amazing that they'll pick your book over thousands of cheaper alternatives.

Another advantage of selling on your own site is being able to bundle your book or books together, bundle them with a course, bundle them with a workbook, and whatever else you've created. This not only allows you to give more value to your customers, you entice those customers to spend a lot more money. This makes your business a lot more fundamentally-sound.

For example, let's say you have a 5-part book series about real estate investing. You have an intro book on becoming a real estate investor, a book on scouting for the best properties, another for knowing how to get the most bang for your buck with renovations, and so on. So, let's say someone stumbles across your first book in the series. They buy it on January 3. They absolutely love it and go on to buy your whole series, giving you roughly $15 in royalties for the purchase of all five books, which you have priced for an average of $4.99.

Well hey, that's pretty awesome. But you don't get that $15 until March 30! That's awfully tough to make your business work. How are you supposed to afford advertising if you have to pay to sell your books, but you don't get your money back from your advertising efforts for up to 90 days!? Moreover, how are you supposed to get someone to buy all five of your books with just a $15 advertising budget? That's not easy to do.

More importantly, think about the customer. It's great to read books about real estate investing, but how much better would it be to also watch videos showing real properties in real time, real renovations, how to stage a home properly, and other things that are best conveyed in video form? Books can only do so much. To really give customers what they want, you have to give them everything they need, and if you can give them everything they need, your products and services are much more valuable.

In contrast, let's say you sell the book series on your website, and you bundle it with a course, a separate buying guide, a series of audio recordings, and a chance to have ongoing email communication with you. This complete package of materials could be sold for $500. You could get quality email subscribers for say, $3-4 each. 2% of them buy your product after subscribing, which is not too terribly hard to do. One of my quasi-proteges, Ari Whitten, just launched a program for increasing your energy levels at that exact price point and crushed it with a 5% conversion rate. Boss!

At a 2% conversion rate, with a $500 product, you'll make $10 per email subscriber, and you'll get it within a week or two of a person subscribing to your email list. Now THAT is a viable business you can make work with relative ease.

Okay, that was a long tangent I know. And many aspiring authors will find all that complicated-sounding business stuff to be like covering your genitals with fire ants, but it would be a disservice not to acknowledge what is a superior way to run a business.

"Hey, I just want to write books. I don't want to get email subscribers or do any coaching, and I certainly don't want to appear on camera."

I get it. But you also have to understand that just writing books is highly disadvantageous when it comes to growing and being truly successful. Publishing on Amazon is also getting more difficult, and book revenues are falling, especially with the advent of their Kindle Unlimited program, which allows readers to read books more cheaply while authors get paid less per book purchased by far. So please, don't shy away from building a real business. It can make or break your ability to succeed, and that's why I'm bringing it to your attention to the point of sounding redundant.

So that's some discussion about selling your books on your own website. The conversation about selling books exclusively on Amazon is a totally different conversation. Every major platform is its own universe. What works on Facebook doesn't necessarily work on Snapchat or YouTube. Amazon is its own universe, and understanding their platform and their goals as a business will help you perform better over there.

Amazon's goal as a business is to monopolize as much that is bought and sold as possible. I think that's pretty clear. They sacrifice profits left and right just to grow and grow with reckless abandon—stealing customers away from as many businesses and industries as possible. They do this mostly by being bigger and better than everyone else at a lower price. It's pretty hard to beat that combination of virtues.

So you know that Amazon wants to sell the most inexpensive books on the face of the planet, making it impossible for other major book vendors to compete. They've been very successful, and they strive to continually give customers more and better books at lower and lower prices. They also want to provide quality books, and they love to emphasize the new and exciting releases. If you are going to be competitive as an author on Amazon, you need to understand this—embrace it fully—and go with the flow. That means you need to write some great books, you need to publish new books often, and you need to be okay with people being able to download your books for practically nothing.

If you've been interested in self-publishing, I'm sure you could find most of what I'm about to say in one of several other books about successful self-publishing. But I doubt you'll hear it put so succinctly.

To be a successful self-publisher on Amazon, in fiction as well as nonfiction (at least in the year 2016, I'm not a psychic), you need to do the following things:

1. **Create a simple author website for collecting the email addresses of your fans**. When you're starting out, the best thing to do is have people submit their email address to get your next release for free, unless you have something else you can give away for free, such as a book you've written that's not published anywhere else, including Amazon, a course, or something else that you think they'd like.

2. **Write and publish a new book every month**. This "book" doesn't have to be long, especially if it's nonfiction. I shoot for 15,000-20,000 words for most of my books. If you are writing fiction, it should be a full-length book that's at least 50,000 words. In addition to these shorter books, I also believe it's good to have a full-length flagship book in your collection as well. Every book you publish should be very professionally-done, clean, and crisp—free of typos and adorned with a professional book cover. If you need help figuring these things out, get in touch with my good friend Rob. He has an inexpensive course on self-publishing for those looking to do everything themselves, and

he also offers a full spectrum of publishing services for those who don't. His website is: www.archangelink.com

3. **Publish your first few books entirely free, focusing on getting as many downloads as you can possibly get.** In both the beginning and the back of your books, invite people to subscribe at your website to get your next release for free or whatever offer you choose. If you do everything correctly, and your books are good, you should see about 3-5% of the people downloading your books making their way onto your mailing list. To truly succeed on Amazon, you need to get dozens of glowing reviews on your book as quickly as possible, and convince their algorithm that your book is popular amongst their users. I believe, for a book to really have a strong chance to be a heavy seller (like, over $10,000 lifetime), you need to get at least 1,000 paid downloads in the first week. To do this, you MUST have a fan base to promote to. If you don't have this fan base, publishing your work for sale is pretty pointless. It just won't get much traction in Amazon's paid store unless you really are a complete badass, or you have other marketing strategies you can rely on (such as a good friend with a really big following on social media willing to share your book, or something like that). So focus entirely on getting your first few thousand email subscribers before you start worrying about making real money.

4. **Once you have a few thousand quality email subscribers or more, begin releasing your books at 99 cents instead of free, raising the price to $2.99 and above after the first week.** The idea is to get the maximum number of paid downloads in the first few days, which increases your ranking, as Amazon's sales rank is based on number of sales, not the dollar amount. What you're doing here is convincing Amazon's algorithm that your book is popular

and in demand. When you do that, you have a chance for your book to really take off and sell well without you having to do anything. It's a hard thing to achieve, but by publishing the best books you can on a regular basis and having an audience already built to get you your first several hundred sales and a dozen amazing reviews, you're setting yourself up to have a good chance at success. You just have to stick with it. Once your audience is big enough to get you 1,000+ paid downloads at launch, you're pretty much unstoppable at that point.

5. **Promote your books on book-promotion sites as much as you can**. They are worth every penny and then some, it's just a matter of being able to secure a spot. It's very competitive, so your book better be good, with solid reviews and a cover that emanates professionalism. There are tons of book-promotion sites out there. www.Bookbub.com is currently the best site by a mile. I've been slacking off on adding new subscribers over the last 18 months with my book promotion site www.BuckBooks.net, but that will be changing soon, and it will be a strong second best like it was in early 2015. The best way to get a promotion spot with Bookbub is to be professional and be persistent. They'll likely turn you down the first few times. Don't give up. The best way to get a guaranteed promotion spot with Buck Books is by getting your book cover done at www.100covers.com.

6. **Reinvest any extra money you make beyond what you need just to survive into getting your Kindle books into print (with Createspace), audiobook (with ACX), and translated into foreign languages.** There is plenty of money to be made in these other formats, particularly audiobooks, which is the fastest growing publishing market in terms of author earnings. Audiobooks make up

about 40% of my total author revenue in the year 2016, whereas they were less than 10% of my total author revenue back in 2013 when I first published them. Print books don't make a ton of money, but it also doesn't cost much to get a book converted to print, and having print options for your readers adds a thick layer of professionalism to your overall author business. Publishing books in other languages (German, French, Portuguese, and Spanish are probably the most common for translations) is a vast topic, but there is tremendous potential out there to make more money off of the work you've already done, and it only stands to improve over time.

7. **Keep writing!** One of the most common mistakes people make is slacking off once they become successful. I know it sounds crazy, but it's true. There are many that use their success to launch other endeavors, which is fine, and quite smart actually, as there is a lot less money in books than there is *outside* of books. But if you're dead set on becoming a career writer, then certainly don't forget to keep doing all the hard work and hustling that you did to become successful once you actually are successful.

What I just described is some really serious work, and it requires so much hard work, determination, and passion that you really must have a strong desire to accomplish it or you'll fizzle out before you even make it to the end of the first year.

One piece of advice I have to share, as I alluded to earlier, is to make sure you want to become a writer because you LIKE WRITING! If you like writing, then you won't have to do much "work." Work, if you define it as "doing something you don't want to do," sucks, and few will do something they dislike long enough to actually get to where they're earning thousands of dollars doing it each month. If you are trying to become a successful writer for other reasons (traveling the world, fame, money), you'll become discouraged pretty quickly when it doesn't deliver any of those things in the first year or two, and you'll move on to something that promises a quicker, easier path to achieving those things.

And once more, just to hit you over the head with it, you'll have a much easier time becoming a successful author, whether you write fiction, nonfiction, or both, if you sell more than just books, and you actually sell something yourself on your own website. As a novelist, this can be tough to envision, but man will it ever make your business more fundamentally sound and easy to scale if you are to sell something exclusive on your own site all bundled with as much stuff as you can think of (video readings of your short stories, a whole awesome series not found on Amazon, signed author copies, etc.).

I mean, if you can just get one out of every ten people who subscribe to your list to spend $39 in a week after they subscribe, then you have a budget of $3.90 to go out and get another subscriber. This can make the difference in having an email list of 2,000 and 200,000, and the difference in you making $2,000 per year or $200,000. Or, more likely, it will make getting to a respectable $50,000 per year in author income (enabling you to quit your job and do it full-time) take ten years instead of one.

So please, do yourself a favor and figure out how to offer more than just books and do it! The rest of the book will have a lot of discussion on what those offerings might be.

Personally, I love publishing books on Amazon AND having lots of other things for sale. Publishing on Kindle is advertising that pays me instead of me paying for advertising. In fact, I published a book one week ago that was released for free for the first 5 days, and I've already collected $270 on one of my websites that's directly related to the book. The book itself has only earned about $12 in royalties so far, which I won't receive from Amazon for 75 more days! With my superior setup, I have $270 to go and advertise my book RIGHT NOW that an author just trying to publish books won't have. You have no idea how huge of an advantage that is. It's a game changer. Really.

Do I have more to say about self-publishing? Man, I could write a 500-pager on self-publishing. It's a vast topic, and it's one that I love. Honestly though, I'm glad I'm limited to just an overview for the purposes of this book though. If I told you everything, you'd likely have too many things to focus on. What I've whittled self-publishing down to here in this chapter is simple. These are the main things you should focus on, as the rest is trivial, and many aspiring authors get lost in the minutiae and never find their way out.

Here's an even simpler version:

Write awesome shit. Publish frequently. Build a list. Start getting sales. Use that money to advertise and expand your offerings into other formats. If at all possible, have some things available for sale on your site to make your business fundamentally healthier. Don't stop!

Good luck writers. I love ya.

Now let's talk about the current craze—courses…

ECOURSES

ECourses are all the rage. Cooking courses, dog training courses (I hear Hung has an outstanding book on crate training puppies!), video editing courses, web design courses, photography courses, investing courses, organic gardening courses, yoga courses, and the list goes on.

Why? I think it's mostly because of the higher perceived value of courses compared to books. It's not much harder to sell a $99 course than it is to sell a $9.99 book.

Over five years ago I was in close communication with the head of a decent-sized blog network. Like most networks, they made most of their money from advertisements—almost like how a magazine makes their money. Most of the bloggers also sold books that they had written, and I use the term "sold" lightly, as no one made a whole lot selling those books. The network was having to put together huge bundles of 50+ books for just $39 or so just to get people to buy them.

But then one of the members of the blog network put together an eCourse. It was a simple course on how to make sourdough bread from scratch or something like that. Nothing too revolutionary.

The network worked together to sell this course, and people were tripping over each other to pay over $100 for a course. The course instructor made a ton of money, and the bloggers did well too, as they all made some pretty decent affiliate commission for promoting the course.

This was my first eye-opener about the power of adding in audio and video and calling something a "course" or "online class" or "program." The perceived value was radically higher, even if the information contained in the course was virtually identical to what could be found in a book.

Think about it. How much do people typically pay for classes? How much do they typically pay for books?

The thing is though, it's not much harder (for most people) to put information into audio and video than it is to put it into a book. From the seller's standpoint, you'd be a fool to put all your great information into a book when you could brand the same information as a "course," spend the exact same amount of time and effort putting it together, and sell it for 10-100x the price.

Remember too that when you sell something at a higher price and earn more money per subscriber, you have a bigger advertising budget, you have something that's a lot more attractive to prospective affiliates who can send you tons of traffic almost overnight, and countless other advantages. Getting more money out of your fans and followers, while it may sound like something only Scrooge McDuck would care about, is pivotal to your ability to expand and really reach people and make a difference, so don't be turned off by it. Your success depends on it. If you really have something great that you think can help benefit others, you should care about your success a lot.

I'd give you some big secrets on how to be successful with online courses, but the big secret with online courses, and why there is a gold rush-esque fever going around the interwebz these days, is that a business that is built around or involves eCourses is easier!

In other words, there's no big secret about eCourses. eCourses ARE the big secret!

But one thing I would suggest is to avoid platforms such as Udemy like the plague, host your course or courses on your own site, and don't try to sell your courses with long copy sales pages. While sales pages still work just fine, it's much wiser to focus solely on building an email list. You don't want affiliates driving traffic to your course's sales page, because only a small percentage (1-10% typically), will actually make an impulse buy and snag your course. 90-99% leave the page and likely never find you again.

Instead, affiliates (and you, through your marketing efforts), should focus on sending traffic to an optin page (as described in the chapter on Email Marketing). This will build up your email list. You'll probably be able to sell not only your course more effectively, but you'll have those email subscribers to promote future courses, book launches, coaching and consulting, a number of different affiliate offers that you come across, and any number of opportunistic ideas that you have in the future. Even promoting a blog post, YouTube video, podcast, or your social media pages to your email subscribers can help the performance of all of those. A big email list can literally make everything you touch turn to gold. Missing those opportunities by focusing on sending people to sales pages is a huge mistake.

For hosting courses on your own site, I recommend using Zippy Courses, a piece of software created by a very successful and experienced internet entrepreneur named Derek Halpern. He's a huge advocate of making courses a big part of your overall internet business. In a recent email to his list he writes…

"There are only 5 types of online business models, and I tried all of them.

And now I can say, without a shadow of doubt, that I love the online course business model the most.

Let me show you why…

You could start selling physical products, but that's going to take inventory. Or manufacturing talent. And that's going to cost a lot to get started.

You could start offering services, and while that's a great business model, the big problem is this: you'll get stuck in the "trading time for project fees" trap and you may never get out of it.

You could launch an online software company, but do you know anything about software? That could get real expensive real quick.

You could rely on paid advertising, but did you know that you'll need MILLIONS of visitors just to make real revenue?

Or…

You could create and sell online courses.

First, I've said it before, and I'll say it again. The online course industry is BOOMING right now. If you look around, you'll see people selling online courses in all different types of industries…

…and in many cases, people are doing real well.

Second, when you create a course the right way, you can create it once, and sell it over and over again for YEARS.

There's no such thing as "doing nothing" and "making a living," but it is possible to front load the work today and reap the benefits for years to come. Online courses can let you do it.

Third, you don't have to drop what you're doing to create and sell online courses full-time. In many cases people often try to build (and sell) a course on the side, and later, when it takes off, they often make it their main priority because "it can scale."

I just had a conversation with a former one-on-one service provider just the other day. He liked helping people one on one, but he told me, quite directly, "It just doesn't scale." But now he focuses on teaching people through online courses because you can help more than one person at a time."

I think that's pretty well-put. Of course, I had to delete his many attempts to get you signed up for his webinar from the above, lol. What's with internet marketers and webinars? Seriously. I know that webinars can be a very powerful way to succeed, but I've left it out of this book because I've always found them to be too cheesy. Stone don't do no webinars. Or anything on camera. Or anything live. That may sound like I have some kind of serious personality disorder, but if you're digitally-free long enough, you'll be completely unable to schedule anything without having a panic attack.

Lastly, before we move on, I wanted to point out the biggest mistake I see with online courses—not being specific enough. I've literally seen courses on "being happy" for sale. Absolutely do NOT create a course that is completely unspecific. Don't be afraid to create a course on a very narrow, pinned-down topic for a very targeted audience.

The first course I ever created was a very specific subject for a very specific audience called "Serious Email List Building for Authors." It was such a niche topic that I had pretty low expectations of making $10,000-20,000 in my initial launch of it. But in the initial launch I did $40,000 and was really happy about that, especially considering that I did it with fewer than 3,000 email subscribers (I ended up making just over $13 revenue per subscriber in a 7-day launch).

What course, class, program, or other educational experience could you create? If you can answer that question with something besides "I don't know," I hope you follow through with it and actually get that course out into the world. Having a course or courses in your bag of tricks can be a powerful tool in expediting your journey to digital freedom.

Now let's jump ahead to one of the most foolproof ways to earn a dependable internet-based income...

COACHING AND CONSULTING

Invariably when I tell someone who is struggling to get beyond $1,000 per month online or thereabouts that they should consider adding coaching/consulting to their online business, they say something like, "I really don't want to spend my time doing one-on-one coaching."

It's a good thing I don't tell this to people in person, because this response would elicit a knee-jerk reaction from me. And when I say "knee-jerk reaction," I literally mean a knee-jerk reaction. My knee would jerk, sending my foot on a swift journey to the epicenter of his or her groin area, toenail to taint.

Listen, no one wants to do coaching and consulting. Well, that's not entirely true. Some people are masochists. What I mean is that no *sane* person would want to do one-on-one coaching. It's kind of fun, but it's extremely draining, and it gets very repetitive. At the end of the day, it's trading time for dollars, and trading time for dollars quickly starts to feel like work, even if you are getting to enjoy the gratification that comes with helping others.

Few who don't HAVE to do coaching and consulting to pay the bills will continue to do it. But we all have to start somewhere, and coaching and consulting can do amazing things for the health of your business. Let me explain why...

Let's say you have a website, and at that website you manage to figure out how to get a steady supply of ten email subscribers per day. This may sound like nothing, but this is plenty of traffic for a good business to succeed. Few, however, have good businesses. They have the virtual equivalent of a Wal-Mart-sized store with one product for sale.

With those ten subscribers, you deliver a series of emails to help sell your flagship course, which costs $100. You manage to get one out of ten to spend $100. Awesome job. That means you're making an average of $100 per day. That's pretty solid for such a small amount of subscribers coming into your pipeline.

But here's what coaching can do…

Of the 10% of people who buy your course, 10% are really fired up about the information they got, and they really connected with you as a person. Trouble is, they just feel a little lost and hesitant about implementing that information. They could really use a coach, a guide, a mentor—and they are willing to pay $1,000 to work with you for an extended period of time until they get on their feet in implementing the sage advice in your course.

With those numbers, an extra $1,000 for every ten people that take your course means that your income goes from $100 per day to $200 per day. Double!

Now you're at $20 RPS instead of $10 RPS, and this can be the difference between being able to scale or not being able to scale.

Now, if you are able to scale with advertising or by launching your own affiliate program, you can go from 10 subscribers per day to 100 subscribers per day. Now you're at $2,000 per day. Of course, at that rate, you are absolutely working your ass into oblivion with all the coaching clients you have (in reality, most will just raise the price of their coaching services, and keep their client load from getting out of hand). But, if you keep that up for a year, you'll manage to build an email list of 36,500.

Once you get there, THEN you can drop the coaching. Your list is big enough to promote various affiliate offers, launch books, launch new courses, launch new websites/ventures, and a variety of other things to replace that coaching income. Or, if you're creative enough, you could even launch a training course to certify individuals to work as one-on-one coaches of your methods on your site, preventing you from having to drop a lucrative coaching wing. These are all things you can't successfully do when your list is too small. That's why you may need to do the coaching starting out.

Yeah, it's hard. I paid my dues—doing hundreds upon hundreds of consultations to grow my very first business (at its peak, consultations were responsible for about a third of my overall monthly revenue). It helped me get where I needed to get, and I believe it can help you, too.

One suggestion I'll make about doing coaching, consulting, or mentoring of some kind is to forbid someone from working with you just one time, or allowing them to add small chunks of time here and there. Rather, you want them to sign up for several sessions for something ongoing at a much higher price point. Get them to commit, and commit to them in return. Make sure the price you charge is something that is worth your personal commitment to them. It should be a price that allows you to absolutely give them your all without feeling like you lost money by focusing on them rather than growing your business.

It may sound absurd or greedy, but I currently charge $10,000 to work intimately with someone to start and grow a successful website, and I'm not at all certain it's a good deal for me at that price. I'm an incredibly generous person that would just about lay my life down to help someone else out. I get help from my whole team to make sure that each person I work with is successful. It distracts all of us to get a mentorship client. We practically groan every time someone drops $10,000. With what we give, and what we give up in terms of time and focus on our businesses to do this kind of work, a fair price is actually more like $20,000-30,000.

I'm no fan of charging up the bazingahole, especially for digital products, which you'll soon discover when you find out more about Digital Freedom Academy at the end of this book. It's an ideological thing, not something that's necessarily governed by statistics (the best small businesses I know are mostly the ones that charge too much). But when it comes to putting your heart and soul and personal time and attention into something 110%? Be very cautious about charging too little, or every minute you spend one-on-one with clients will eat away at your soul. Charge an amount that makes you happy to get a new client, and not a penny less. It will be good for your morale, and your morale is important. It will determine the quality of the experience that you'll be able to deliver to your coaching clients.

Lastly, before we move on from the topic of coaching and consulting, I wanted to mention two of the biggest mistakes I see—both mistakes are on the same coin. One mistake is thinking that you need to be some major heavy duty expert about something in order to provide coaching and consulting and charge appropriately for it. You don't have to be the world's preeminent authority on something to be valuable to someone looking to improve their lives in some way. You should be familiar, and you should have some practice at coaching people through whatever process you profess to be knowledgeable about, but you don't have to be a celebrity or have a Nobel Prize or anything like that.

The other mistake is thinking that you do have expertise and offering up coaching and consulting services when you really don't! I know that may seem contradictory, but many individuals have a really hard time estimating their worth. You see it all the time with things like *American Idol* auditions, where it seems the least talented think they are the next Adele, and the most talented are often completely shocked and floored that the judges like them.

This misjudging of one's value, worth, expertise, and ability to guide others with one-on-one guidance is a common mistake, but not one that I have a remedy for. Hopefully bringing it to your awareness will at least get you thinking more critically about which camp you most likely fall into— the humble genius or the entitled wannabe.

I bring this up because I don't want anyone with real talent and expertise hindering their business by being afraid of doing some kind of high-priced coaching, nor do I want to encourage someone who just watched their first Guy Kawasaki video last Tuesday to start giving out expensive financial advice. Know what I mean, Vern?

Okay, moving on…

SUBSCRIPTIONS

A subscription to some kind of ongoing content or service is a fabulous way to make money online. While I always love to get money up front—gathering it quickly so I can recycle it back into advertising and scale—a subscription with a monthly, quarterly, semi-annual, or annual fee provides the luxury of *steady* income. Steady income is an extreme rarity when it comes to earning internet-based income, and it's that lack of consistency that really makes quitting your day job so damn scary. I mean, what use is digital freedom if you're worried about where your income is going to come from every month?

I personally have sold several subscription-based products…

Coinciding with that very first sloppy book I mentioned earlier on was the sale of a $97 annual subscription to a monthly eZine that I created. Those were the first two products I started with online.

Later on I started a subscription-based site called 180 Radio, an offshoot of my website 180DegreeHealth. While I failed to get other people involved with 180 Radio like I had hoped, it worked out pretty gloriously for me. After six months or so I had over 700 paying subscribers paying $2.99/month. Not an outrageous amount of money, but it was pretty good considering all I did for it was put out 3-4 podcasts per month.

What are some subscription-based products and services that you could offer? I can think of several that I could offer just off the top of my head.

Because I have so much experience on the internet with such a wide variety of things, my brain is inundated with great business ideas all the time. All of them would be viable enough for someone to make a great living from their pajamas, but I don't execute any of them because my team is already scattered around enough with the avalanche of ideas I've thrown at them. I could easily start a subscription-based service where I go over these business ideas in detail as they come to me every month.

I currently do what I call a monthly "State of the Interwebz" address for a select group of people, where I go over the things I'm doing in my business, sharing ideas, and more—and that could have easily been a subscription-based service, I just chose not to go that route with it.

Just about any "course" could become a subscription if it's something that's conducive to frequent updates with new information.

Of course, eZines are the most common—where people subscribe to get a monthly online magazine.

Digital Freedom Academy is like a big Thrive Market for aspiring digital entrepreneurs. Thrive Market is an internet-based business that operates a lot like Costco. You pay an annual fee, and that annual fee allows customers to shop around and buy great products at wholesale prices. With Digital Freedom Academy, your fees allow you to access tons of books, courses, and other premium resources for FREE. No fees at all beyond the cost of the subscription. Or at least, that's what it will be when it officially launches in late

November of 2016. Maybe you could come up with something like that in your area of interest.

This may not be much concern to you now, but another benefit of a subscription-based product or service is that, with consistent revenue and profits, and a track record of steady, reliable growth and customer retention, your business is infinitely more attractive to potential buyers should you ever choose to sell it. That's something I think about a lot, as I'm always starting more websites than I can manage. My sites have a tendency to peak and then get neglected, and I would be much better off handing the keys over to someone else who can give them the love they deserve.

Are subscriptions special? I don't think so. I don't think subscription-based products and services are flat out superior than selling products and services outright, but I want you to strongly consider adding a subscription-based product or service to your game plan.

The reason, once again, is creating a more fundamentally-sound business. A business that just sells books, for example, is a bad business. I made reference earlier to most online businesses being crappy businesses—the equivalent to a Wal-Mart-sized store with only one product on the shelves.

A better "store" is one with lots of products at lots of different price points to meet the needs of a lot of people. When you have that, people buy more stuff, and when people buy more stuff, the average amount they pay goes up. That means a lot, because getting a decent amount of money out of the email subscribers you get determines whether you can have enough extra money to hire people to help you grow, pay for advertising, create a decent affiliate program that pays enough to get people spreading the word about your products and services, and so on.

And that's why adding a subscription to go along with books, courses, coaching, and whatever else you can think of to sell (perhaps an annual conference ticket, t-shirts, physical products, services, various affiliate offers that you think your audience will like, and the list goes on), increases your chances of success. I call businesses that take advantage of having multiple revenue streams like that "complete businesses." Complete businesses are easy to make successful.

I think the hardest thing to do online is to draw a lot of regular, quality traffic to a site. Making more money per site visitor enables you to make a living without having to depend on a huge truckload of visitors to earn a decent income. You don't have to be famous and "break the internet" with something that goes viral to eek out a living. You can do it with as few as 20 quality visitors to a solid lead page per day.

THAT is doable, and figuring out how to do such a thing is what got me so excited to reach out and educate as many people as possible. Success online and a life of boundless freedom isn't just for people like Tim Ferriss. Regular people can totally do it, too.

Well I went and totally blew my load early. There's a first time for everything I guess! Let me get back out of Tony Robbins mode and finish this book. There are still a ton of other ways to earn a dependable living online that we haven't discussed yet...

PODCASTING

Podcasting is yet another fine way to make a living online. I'm not the best talker, and I'm the absolute worst listener (I have a pathological inability to care what anyone else thinks!), so I never really got very into podcasting personally. Still, I did manage, as I mentioned earlier, to get people to subscribe to listen to a private podcast of mine, and quickly got that up over $2,000 per month before killing it shortly thereafter and pursuing other opportunities. But that's not how people typically make money with podcasting. Not at all.

Podcasters start out making no money at all. But, if you manage to start a podcast and stick with it until it's getting some traction, you can start making money by advertising—just how people in radio make money. Having an audience of loyal listeners is a check waiting to be cashed similarly to how attracting a bunch of traffic with a blog creates countless opportunities to make money.

It's not *Field of Dreams*, where you build it and they will come. But if you build it and they do come, the money will come with it.

What I don't like about podcasting is that it takes a really long time to reach the point of success—usually several years. Growth, while it's usually exponential, takes an eternity to gather momentum. With no audience, you have very little ability to draw great guests, and without being able to draw in great guests, it's hard to get going. Most that attempt to make it in podcasting never get out of neutral.

Just like with blogging, you also have to become REALLY huge in podcasting to make a great living. You'll be lucky to get more than a couple cents per podcast download in advertising dollars—meaning that you'll need 150,000 downloads per month just to reach $3,000 per month.

However, there are some perks of podcasting that I absolutely love:

One is that podcasting pretty much forces you to go outside of your comfort zone and build relationships with other people in your niche (not all podcasts are built around interviews, but most are because podcasters typically need to piggyback on the success of others to build a fan base from scratch). Getting to know the people in your niche, and them getting to know you as well, is a very valuable thing. Those relationships that you build—and those relationships are usually very strong since you are actually speaking with the person one-on-one in a phone interview—can later lead to promotional partnerships and a variety of other mutually-beneficial endeavors.

Take for example my relationship with a guy named Tom Corson-Knowles. Tom originally invited me to be a guest on his health podcast. I said yes and we had a great conversation. I sent several hundred clicks over to check out the interview, which helped him get exposure.

About a year later, when I was doing some research for the launch of Archangel Ink with my buddy Rob (a company that helps self-published authors), I happened to notice that Tom had some books about self-publishing, a course about self-publishing, and a business helping self-publishers that was very similar to what we were hoping to build.

I reached out to Tom and told him what we were doing, and told him that we were offering something he didn't—audiobook production. We did an audiobook for one of his clients for free so he could test it out and see how it sold.

Sure enough, it sold pretty well just as we predicted, and Tom sent us over dozens of audiobook projects in just a few months, which brought us thousands of dollars a month right from the start. He further helped us out by promoting and publicizing my book promotion site Buck Books when that launched in May of 2014. I then promoted tons of Tom's books through Buck Books. Tom then launched a product called Bestseller Ranking Pro and I promoted that for him. I made money promoting it, and he made more money from the promotion. I also introduced him to Derek Murphy and Steve Scott who promoted Tom's stuff as well.

And all that collaboration that has led to countless thousands of extra dollars made by both of us started with just a simple podcast! And we've only known each other for four years. We've probably got many more years of mutually-beneficial collaborations ahead of us.

Because of that, I think you have to look beyond the advertising dollars when it comes to podcasting. Podcasting is a simply amazing tool to network with others, and networking with others is one of the most powerful tools to being successful online. The internet is all about *collaboration*, not competition.

Another perk of podcasting is that you are getting people to actually take time to listen to in-depth conversations of yours. This is really high-quality, intimate exposure. This high-quality exposure tends to form more personal, loyal bonds with your followers than written articles and sharing memes on social media and stuff like that. And with those loyal bonds comes much greater trust and respect—the kind that makes launching new products and services to instant success a breeze. It also makes promoting the products of others a breeze, turning you into the type of person who everyone wants to help and be helped by—another powerful asset.

So, as much as I dislike the actual activity of producing a podcast, and as much as I detest the long period of time it takes to become successful (I think quick success is the most important single factor, as the most common cause for failure with internet business is giving up because it takes too long to earn a living—so that's a huge strike against podcasting), I do have a lot of positive things to say about it.

What's the formula for success? What tips do I have to share? I'd say most of the tips I gave for becoming a successful blogger apply to becoming a successful podcaster. You have to have flamboyant personality (be bold!), you want to spend at least as much time trying to publicize your content as you spend creating it, you want to network with others, and you want to be relentlessly prolific and consistent.

But I have a tip to share here that trumps all of that, and I think it can eliminate what is by far the biggest downer about podcasting, which is the lengthy process of gaining traction in the beginning. Want to become a successful podcaster in a matter of months instead of years? No problem. Don't put your audio recordings into a "podcast" on iTunes. Instead, make 30-50 or so recordings with the best people you can get, and put it all into an "online summit."

The way these work is that the summit organizer will create a simple optin page where the public can access the interviews for free in exchange for an email address. Each participant in the summit is expected to drive as much traffic as possible over to this page, so that the event organizer can gather tens of thousands of email addresses in just a matter of weeks.

Now, usually the audio recordings are only temporarily available, which makes listening to them all virtually impossible (Is that why they are called "virtual" summits? Haha). The subscriber is then bludgeoned repeatedly about buying all of the recordings (for $97-199 usually), so they can listen to all of the interviews on their own time. When a sale occurs, the affiliate that referred the subscriber (usually one of the participants), gets 50-75% of that.

But nobody buys them. Maybe they did back in the day, but these virtual summits are so widespread, and the gimmick so overdone, that it just doesn't work very well anymore. Of course, as the summit organizer, you don't care too much as long as you got your subscribers and all that instant exposure. But you should care, because everyone's collective inability to sell these summits means that the participants quickly get jaded, and they either don't bother sending traffic over your way (wasting all your efforts, as your recordings will be heard by absolutely no one!), or they refuse to participate altogether.

What is a better way? A better way is to truly allow everyone to access the interviews for free without being gimmicky or obnoxious, and then pitch something for sale that is of more value once the summit has concluded (like books, courses, coaching, a subscription to something, and so on). Once again, to reference Self-Publishing School, they host a summit each year and give the participants 40% of the Self-Publishing School sales that occur after those leads have been gathered, paying up to $800 for referring the lead. That's what I'm talkin' about. They sell it pretty effectively, too.

I personally would probably give participants a guaranteed $1 per email subscriber they refer, so they know they'll get paid for referring traffic whether the leads buy something from me or not. Again, that's risky and not something a total newb should carelessly promise, but with dozens of ways to make money from an email list and a decade of experience, it's no risk for me to offer $1. I can make $1 per subscriber giving away free stuff! I don't even need to sell them anything!

Well that pretty much wraps up the conversation on podcasting. Now onto to discuss one of my favorite platforms...

YOUTUBE

People make money on YouTube? You betcha. While trying to make it big on YouTube is ridden with the same problems that make podcasting or blogging a long journey to success (unless you make prank videos), I think the formula for reaching success there is pretty straightforward, and the chances of being successful are very high for any relatively sane person willing to put in the work.

YouTubers get paid primarily from advertisement income. Yep, those completely obnoxious ads that we all can't seem to close or skip fast enough, actually pay the bills for thousands and thousands of people. Who these people are that actually pay attention to these ads, I have no clue. But on behalf of YouTubers everywhere, we thank you.

Have I made it big on YouTube? No I have not. But I've had over 1 million views on my videos, which is enough to make a few thousand bucks had I enabled those annoying ads (which I didn't, because I'm cool like that). And I'm sure I could have made far more than that had I panhandled my audience for support on Patreon, a tactic I'll discuss in the next chapter.

And while 1 million views isn't very much, keep in mind that I haven't made a video in like four years, and the only time I really consistently tried to grow my following on YouTube lasted only a few months before I ditched it for better opportunities (I'm not all that gifted on camera, and I was slightly pudgy and discussing health and nutrition, which is, well, not a good time let's say). Yet I still get video views every day on several channels (my QuitN6, 180Degree-Health, and mnobeyed channels).

In all, I made about 200 videos I think. So what's that, 5,000 views per video and roughly $15-20 per video made in would-be advertising income? It's not bad really. And my visibility there led to books and courses sold and probably an additional $10,000-20,000 all told, which is more like $50-100 per video. Not too shabby, as I spent less than an hour on average per video recorded and uploaded (although, admittedly, that's pretty half-assed, and a properly recorded and edited video with love should take twice that long or more).

Honestly, I think just about every teenager on earth should have one or more YouTube channels, and they should upload videos there in their spare time, accumulating hundreds if not thousands of videos by the time they reach adulthood. It challenges them to be creative, to communicate, and to actually build something. It will also give them their first taste of making money doing something fun, exciting, and free. This money doesn't simply dry up when you stop making videos either. After you've made the videos, the advertising income you receive is purely passive—pretty helpful when you're trying to really figure out what you want to do with your life and don't have any skills worth more than minimum wage.

So yeah, get on YouTube and start cranking them out.

What's the formula for success over there? Once again, the success formula is a lot like the success formula that I laid out for blogging. Be bold, spend as much time sharing your content as you do making it, network with others, and be relentlessly prolific and consistent.

With YouTube, making really great videos that you spend a ton of time on is a great tactic. Good quality videos usually do really well over there. But you don't HAVE to be a video wiz to succeed. You can get in front of the camera and talk about something and upload a sloppy video every damn day and be successful, too. Both can work, because income on YouTube is primarily about video views. The more videos you have, the more views you get. If you manage to get 10,000 subscribers let's say, then releasing a video every day will get you thousands of views automatically just in the first few days from your ongoing audience, and boom, that's worth $10 right away and brings in a small amount of pocket change every day after for eternity.

What you make videos about makes a big difference on You-Tube as well. It doesn't take much time spent on YouTube to figure out what gets an insane amount of views. Just with blogging, celebrity gossip, current events, health and fitness, cooking, and other things that you'll see in any supermarket checkout aisle are big on YouTube. It's just what the masses are into.

Being controversial helps over there as well. People make a killing when they call out other big YouTubers and shoot down their ideas, opinions, etc. Stuff like that stirs up a huge ruckus over there. The greatest master of that tactic is, without question, a guy named Vegan Gains, whose rise to popularity happened as quickly as anyone I've ever witnessed. He basically just trolls the shit out of every big YouTuber, and the YouTubers get so mad they can't help but make a video about it, and the next thing you know the whole argument draws a huge audience and goes viral. He's going to end up getting around 100 million views in his first two years on YouTube, which is well beyond 6-figures per year in advertising income.

Pranks and humor of all kinds are absolutely huge. People have made millions by having the courage to do silly things to strangers, their significant others, their parents, etc.

Acts of inspiring kindness are huge, too, if mean pranks aren't your thing. People get tons of views by giving out gifts to strangers, giving gifts to the homeless, and other random acts of kindness. People love to watch human reactions to uncommon situations and events. One of my favorite videos shows the reactions of deaf people when they are getting to hear for the first time. It's pretty much the best video of all time, as it inspires me to tears AND one of the deaf girls is absurdly hot. That always gets me. Damn you girls and all your hotness.

Let's not forget random acts of cuteness as well! Buy some puppies and kittens and just follow those little furry bastards around with a camera. You'll be in the money in no time!

Anything about sex is a plus, and I don't mean making porn over there. Videos about sex, picking up girls, kissing strangers, and impressive displays of attractiveness—it's all pure gold on YouTube. Just being moderately attractive and making videos about what you ate or what you did today can make you a pretty well-paid YouTube celebrity in short order.

And that brings up what is probably the biggest advantage that YouTube has over all other ways to make money online. You don't have to be an expert that dishes out advice and wisdom. You don't have to be a creative artist that writes gripping 500-page novels. Hell, you can be a total dumbass and just film yourself eating large quantities of disgusting things. I've watched more L.A. Beast videos than I care to admit! The dude ate a raw cactus. Clearly he deserves to be paid well!

The biggest YouTuber of all? He records himself playing video games with the foulest, most vulgar commentary you can imagine. No talent there.

It's true, I love YouTube. And YouTube loves those who consistently make videos. If you have no idea what to do for a business, and you're not an expert on anything, then fire up the ol' video camera and get started. It's a lot of fun.

And I have what I think can more than double your You-Tube earnings without much effort on your part at all. I discuss that next...

DONATIONS

Want to get a little extra revenue out of your fans to help make your business more fundamentally-sound and scalable?

Opposed to the whole capitalist, businessy, salesy vibe altogether and just want to give all your stuff away to the world for free—never SELLING anything—but still make a living from helping or entertaining people?

Want to distinguish yourself from other money-hungry people in your niche by showing that you're not all about the money?

Hate advertising other people's garbage and promoting affiliate crap with your popularity and wish you could find another way to monetize the following you've built with your blog, podcast, social media following, or YouTube channel?

Regardless of your motivations, accepting donations or allowing people to pay what they want or offering a sliding scale to keep your services accessible to po' folks and other innovative techniques, is something to strongly consider.

I'm a huge fan of stepping outside of the typical capitalistic model and hitting people over the head with unexpected authenticity, sincerity, and genuineness in the form of donation-based monetization.

Not selling stuff and asking instead for voluntary financial support doesn't mean taking a vow of poverty either. The most successful "sales" email I've ever written gets 39% of the people who open the email to click on the Buy Now button at the bottom. The secret is simply offering up a very equitable pricing scheme that allows people to choose their own price, or in my case, choosing their own coupon code.

You should really check out what I've done (as Buck Flogging) to get some innovative ideas for how you can stand out with something radical and different, too. It's email #2 that you get after subscribing at: QuitN6.com.

That may seem like a shameless plug, but it's not. I just want you to see that email. I think you'll agree that it's pretty badass.

Another way to easily handle making donation-based income is to ask your fans and followers to support you on www.Patreon.com.

I haven't used the service before, but when I was first turned onto it I was floored. It's a phenomenal idea, and a great, official way to have your online income handled. I think it's truly one of the neatest things on the internet for people looking to do something cool and get paid for it without being douchey. It's up there with things like Kickstarter.

My understanding is that the site encourages your supporters to sign up for a monthly payment to give you ongoing funds to keep doing whatever it is that you're doing. It's a no-brainer for artists, bloggers, YouTubers, and podcasters who otherwise make their money mostly from advertising, but I think it would be effective for freelancers, educators, coaches, writers, and more.

Plus, there's just something particularly fulfilling about knowing that people feel so grateful that you exist and do what you do that they are compelled, purely out of goodwill, to drop a few bones every month to keep you and your family fed and clothed.

And you know, that whole dependability thing that comes from a steadily-rising recurring income.

I don't have any big tips on how to do this in the most tasteful and effective way. I personally don't like the word "donation" and its connotation. It conjures up thoughts of evil entities seducing the general public with the emotionality of an important "cause," only to take the funds raised and channel them over to drug companies to produce ineffective and dangerous drugs for profit and call them a "cure."

But words like "support" resonate. I also suspect that promising certain things at various benchmarks would be really helpful, such as a band promising to launch a tour at a certain funding level, a blogger promising to take the time and money to publish a killer book when funding reaches a certain level, and so on.

I also suspect that continuing to be unexpectedly kind and cool, answering personal emails from fans, and interacting with them intimately without ever asking for anything in return will create exponentially more reciprocation. Being successful with a donation-based model, as with actually selling things successfully, is all about creating trust and making connections. You do that, and you'll definitely make money online. Doing it via donations just might be a way that uniquely strengthens your brand and makes you feel warmer and fuzzier when you get into bed at night.

So give that some thought. It may be a perfect way for you to make a living.

Before moving on, I should note that it doesn't have to be the ONLY way you earn either. I could see a choice being very effective, where you sell a course for $99 or so and say something like:

"If you can't afford that, I totally understand. There have been plenty of times in my life when I couldn't spare that. No need to risk getting evicted to take my course! I'm still happy to allow you to take the course if you can support me on Patreon.com. You can do that for as little as $5/month, and if you do you'll get instant access to the course."

Alrighty then, let's now discuss a huge category of online earning potential—providing a service of some kind...

SERVICES

You're wanting to provide a service in exchange for money on the internet? What kind of sick, punishment glutton are you? Don't you know you actually have to do WORK to do well!!??

I'll be the first to admit from my experiences in trying to have a successful run with Archangel Ink, that running a service-based business is a lot more work for a lot less reward than say, trying to sell courses. Refer back to the quote earlier in the book by Derek Halpern to get a taste of why I (and all people who don't get pleasure from intense pain) feel that way.

You aren't particularly "free," as you are typically on someone else's time and schedule. You don't know when the clients are going to come in and when they'll disappear, the amount of communication required is typically outrageous for the amount of money exchanged, clients are like a box of chocolates in terms of what it's like to deal with them day in and day out, and all things considered it's almost like being a realtor. You're never at work, but always working.

Providing services is also ridiculously competitive. It seems every citizen of every developing country is out there competing for work and willing to do just about anything you ask for five bucks. Then you have Elance (or Odesk or whatever it's called this week), guru.com, and several other hubs for freelancers to recklessly take the going price of any and all services rendered over the internet down to crumbs.

I know I sound negative. I mean, it's almost like I buried this tiny chapter towards the end of the book because service-based businesses are so ugh!

But don't let me turn you away completely. I do have some good news about freelancing and creating a service-based business of some kind, and some strategies that work a lot better than entering the freelancer mosh pit on one of the popular freelancer hubs. Man I hate those places.

Firstly, what are some services you could provide to people on the internet? Pretty much anything you can think of really. You could do graphic design, record yourself reading something for people, create animated videos, do custom artwork, create jingles for small businesses, edit videos, proofread books and blog posts—or write the entire thing, do some bookkeeping, run someone's social media pages for them, write legal contracts, and the list goes on eternally.

Anything that you can learn how to do to the point of doing it better than the average person can lead to a successful service-based business. Also, anything you are willing to do that others might not want to do or have time to do can lead to a successful service-based business. And anything innovative, creative, helpful, or even just entertaining can be the foundation of a successful service-based business. The sky's the limit. And for that reason, service-based businesses, as hard as they are to run, are an option for hundreds of thousands that are currently overworked and underpaid as a pawn in someone else's creation. Let's talk about them...

Rule #1 (there's only one rule, relax) is definitely to stop thinking of yourself as a "freelancer" and start thinking about starting, owning, and running a business. Trying to be a freelancer is like jumping in the water with piranhas. Don't do it. There are too many fish in the sea doing slave work for too little money to get in there and try to compete shoulder to shoulder.

You're also completely insane if you think you can go onto one of those big freelancer sites and have clients find you. If you insist on being a mere mortal freelancer in the true sense, at least go find your own clients. Don't wait for them to come to you. Not only will you work for someone you like (you are reaching out to them specifically because you like them and want to work for them), but you won't spend over half your time communicating with prospective clients—trying to swoon them with samples and testimonials and big discounts and whatever else it takes to get them to pick you instead of the other 30 people who do exactly the same thing you do.

Believe me. Rob and I once went out looking for new audio-book narrators on one of the big freelancer platforms. We posted what we were looking for, and within 48 hours we had over 60 personal replies. We had multiple exchanges and samples sent over from dozens of freelancers, and at the end of the long, drawn out process we ended up working with just four of them. Of the four, only two of them have gotten a large quantity of consistent work from us over the past couple of years since our freelancer fishing trip (One of them is narrating this part right now, which is weird. I think this book just became way too self-aware for those who decided to go with the audio version).

In other words, 58 other freelance voiceover artists wasted anywhere from a few minutes to as much as an hour for absolutely nothing, and this happens again and again in the viciously competitive freelancer world. It's a huge waste of time and talent that could be spent actually doing the craft that these people are wanting to get paid to do!

Back to the idea of thinking like a business owner instead of a freelancer, I strongly suggest building an entity that is expandable. Let's say you are an expert on health and nutrition, and you start doing some ghostwriting. You reach out to a few of your favorite health experts on YouTube who don't have any books published (or maybe the one they do isn't very good), and propose to write something for them. You get a few gigs and write some killer books for them. They're really impressed, and they are able to sell their books really well and get a ton of positive feedback for them. They then request a whole series of books and for you to also start a blog for them.

That's more work than you can handle. Plus, they have told a couple of other people about your service, and you're now getting queries from them. But after writing several books for several people you're already getting a little burnt out. You also know that there are 200-300 other viable candidates in the health and nutrition space alone that could take advantage of having some help writing books, blogs, and other online content to better leverage their popularity.

If you think like a business owner instead of a freelancer, you can start hiring out a team of experienced writers and instead play the role of editor to make sure everything going to clients is up to your high standards. You pay them half of everything you collect, but it allows you to take on six times as many clients and make three times as much moolah.

Then you think of all the opportunities beyond just the health and nutrition space. You hire a good editor to take your place and give them a cut. Meanwhile, you are still collecting more money than you did working like crazy as a freelancer, and your team is doing all the work for you while you go out and expand your team and your company's reach even further, building a REAL business with 7-figure potential, all-the-while avoiding getting mired in doing all the repetitive writing yourself.

That's why it's better to brand your company as a service rather than to market yourself as a freelancer. A freelancer can only go so far, and from what I've seen, all freelancing eventually leads to burnout. Plus, it's actually a lot easier to build a business that provides a service than it is to go it alone, entering the freelancer gauntlet as a lone wolf.

Against my better judgment, I'm actually helping someone build a book cover design service right now (late summer of 2016). The book cover design space is a classic example of a bunch of lone freelancers scrambling around out there for business. There is a ton of talent out there, but ultimately a cover design service called something like "Jessica Johnson Book Covers" just doesn't have the same gravity as an entity with a clear purpose and objective in the market.

The design service is called <u>100 Covers</u> (100 as in $100), and it's distinguishing itself as the perfect middle-of-the-road option between the freelance professionals charging $300-1,000+ for custom book cover design, and the barely literate hacks over at Fiverr making hideous, templated book covers for under $100. I don't think either option is a smart business decision for an author (one option is too low in quality and the other is just too expensive and risky since most self-published books, great cover or not, make less than $1,000 lifetime), so I felt this service was desperately needed in the rapidly-growing self-publishing space.

One designer will be doing all the covers to start (she's done some great work in the past and even did the cover on a perennial Amazon bestseller—it was published over two years ago and sits in the top 100 Kindle books in all of nonfiction), but if she gets overloaded it will be a breeze to bring in quality designers one at a time and expand infinitely. I think it has a lot of potential, I just hope she knows the can of worms she's opening by starting a labor-heavy service-based business!

I don't have a ton of tips for being successful with a service-based business, but I have a few that I think will help you a lot…

1. **Be willing to work your ass off for cheap or even free for a few months to a year to build some traction in the space you're entering into.** Traditionally, in business, making your first profit in year 5 of operations is considered "good." I don't think you have to be that archaic in your thinking, but don't be too short-sighted either. Like Elon Musk said about Tesla in 2016 (I'm paraphrasing), "Yeah, we hope to report our first profit this year. But you know, I'm not gonna like, sacrifice GROWTH just to report a profit (chuckle)." Growing and getting your name out there is an asset that can be cashed in on later. Don't try to strike it rich right away. Get the word out, build a reputation, build some reciprocity, and the money will come.

2. **Identify your ideal clients and actually reach out and offer to do some work for those clients!** Like I said earlier, you want to reach out to clients, not wait for them to come to you—at least not when you're getting started. Get out there and put your talents and desire to do quality work that matters on display!

3. **Network strategically with the right people.** Identify the people who are in touch with your ideal customers

(talking about the big bloggers, YouTubers, etc. in the space you're offering services), and reach out offering to do them a HUGE favor of some kind—potentially even provide services to them for free. I was able to build a service-based business practically overnight by doing this (remember the part about my friend Tom Corson-Knowles?). Building a good relationship with people who are respected authorities in communication with thousands of your ideal clients can save you years of scurrying around trying to stir up some work.

That's all I have to say about service-based businesses. While it may be more work starting out, and running a service-based business can be much more complicated and tricky to scale, for hardworking people-pleasers who genuinely love helping others, internet-based service businesses provide infinite opportunities to achieve digital freedom.

PHYSICAL PRODUCTS

I'll be the first to admit that I'm no physical products expert. One thing I can say though, is that I have studied the digital-based physical products sector for a long time with great excitement. I just don't think it's for me, and I've already got my spoon in too many pots as you've gathered by this point!

Having said that, my dad is literally just launching his first FBA (Fulfillment by Amazon) private label product the month this book is being written. I was the one who originally turned him onto the idea, as I could clearly see the massive potential there (several of my close online amigos, such as Chris Guthrie, were having almost instant success with FBA). The dude is obsessed. He won't shut up about it.

And that's because it really is exciting, and, while complex with a steep learning curve, selling private-label products on Amazon can be very lucrative. Like, stupid money. There's enough potential there that my dad was eager and willing to divert tons of time and attention away from big money-makers in his life (he's a 6-figure consultant and like, a part owner of a fricking AIRLINE!) to take a crack at it.

The quick overview of how it works for those who are totally uninitiated to it, is as follows…

1. Do a ton of research to find a good product to sell (competing products have high sales volume, competition is low/not too crowded)

2. Find a private label product that you can sell. Private label products are basically products that are already made that you can buy at wholesale prices, give your own branding to, and sell at a higher price.

3. Release the thing at a low price to get a ton of sales and reviews and move up in the ranks. You know how Amazon works (if you paid attention to the chapter on self-publishing!). Just like with books, it's important to achieve a high sales rank to convince their algorithm that your product is in demand, and you need lots of quality reviews and a great-looking listing for your product to become a perennial seller.

4. Monitor inventory levels and know when to reorder from the company that makes your product.

5. Try some advertising (on Amazon itself... Advertising directly to people who are currently shopping is pretty epic) to see if you can boost performance even further.

6. Rinse and repeat.

7. Hope your product or products sell so well that Amazon buys your product and/or entire company from you—they pay WELL (like 8-10 times annual profit, which is more than double for what typical websites sell for).

Note, at no point do you really even have to touch the product. The company will ship inventory with your private label on it to Amazon. Amazon will send it to customers. They deposit funds into your bank account every month.

A little daunting sure, but it's doable, and the success rate for those doing this (at least in 2016), is still very high. The opportunity to get in and do well is far from peaking, and Amazon's growth as a company is meteoric and a long way from losing momentum.

Like I said though, I'm no expert, but Hung and I do hope to provide excellent information via a REAL expert on the Digital Freedom Academy website by 2017 for those interested in testing the waters. So stay tuned and keep your fingers crossed that we can land something really great to host on the site for our members to check out.

While Amazon is the hottest and most exciting place to be selling physical products, it's certainly not the only place to sell.

Remember that eBay place from way back when? Turns out it still exists (currently the #7 ranked site in the U.S.), and having success over there, and quick success at that, is as close to a sure thing as you'll find when it comes to making a dependable internet-based income.

Two guys that I hired to start a website (PaleoDork.com) told me recently that they got their start online with eBay. I had no idea, but sure enough they did. And one of them was really adamant that it was a great place for newbies to start out online, and I think he's absolutely right. It's a good place to have quick success, build some confidence, and catch the fever of jobless income. After spending the last year as an internet business educator for the first time, I can't tell you how important those three factors are. They're everything.

That guy (I can't tell you his name, as his current employer has already fired several people for having "side hustles"—reason #457 why even high-paying jobs are bullshit!) is building a course right now called "$100 a Day the eBay Way," and we too hope to be able to share that with our beloved Freedom Seekers over at DFA when it's ready. The dude has a cushy 6-figure job and is a prestigious sportswriter, so I'm not holding my breath that he'll make room in his schedule to hammer this out. But here's to hopin'.

While being a seller on eBay is about the least glamorous way to make a living online, I think it's the perfect opportunity for someone who doesn't already have a bunch of kickass skills and/or expertise in something and who can't quite figure out what else to do online.

And then, last but not least in the physical product realm, is Etsy. Tons of people have made great money making and selling their own homemade artisanal products on Etsy. I think this is an awesome way to turn a hobby into a source of income—potentially even an awesome source of income—and is one of the best ways for people who hate being on the computer to still get a taste of digital freedom.

Etsy is a pretty cool platform with a strong ethical backbone that is hard not to like, and it's no joke either. As I'm typing this they are the #39 ranked website in the entire United States. They're no Amazon or eBay, but there are still plenty of people doing plenty of shopping over there. With a unique product or products that are well-made and in alignment with the general artsy, wholesome, organic vibe over there—and consistent effort towards raising awareness about the product—I'm sure Etsy can be a viable way to earn an internet-based living. My 11-year old "daughter" (girlfriend's daughter, technically), loves to carve wood, and I could see her doing great over there in several years if and when she truly masters her craft.

Unfortunately, Etsy is where my knowledge is most lacking. I've got more inspiration than insight to share about how to be successful, but, just as with Amazon and eBay, Hung and I hope to provide quality insider information from a real expert as soon as we can get our hands on it.

Well folks, we're getting close to the end (obviously, I've been talking out my ass for the whole chapter here!), but I've got one more topic to discuss before I return to my unproductive slacker ways. It's also something I know little about, but am very fired up about personally, as it's the next frontier I aim to conquer...

SITE-FLIPPING

Geez. I can finally talk about what I—ME—am currently having bouts of insomnia over on a regular basis. It's about time!

First of all, I really hate the term "site-flipping." Makes me think of sleazeballs trying to turn a quick buck back in the real estate bubble of the 2000's. That doesn't describe the subject I'm wanting to discuss at all, which is merely selling websites once you've gotten them going.

I love starting websites, but when I see flaws in them that I know will keep them from being 8-figure sites, I'm quick to move on to the next site that corrects the mistakes of the last one. In that process, the original website, which was doing just fine, gets neglected in pursuit of those really big ideas. I mean, making a living online is great, but I'm beyond that stage and onto the "let's see if we can create something really big and awesome" phase, more for fun than for any other reason. I'm not a materialist at all. It's more like progressing through the levels in Super Mario Bros. I was psyched to make it to the level where Mario is swimming around in the water, but a few rounds of that and it's time to move on to saving the princess.

And for that reason, I know I'm the perfect candidate for starting sites with a bang and then selling them if they don't feel like "the one."

While I have yet to actually sell a site, the process seems to have been made extremely simple by Joe Magnotti and Justin Cooke at Empire Flippers. They boast a 95% success rate in selling the sites that they choose to list for sale. They currently charge a $297 fee to list your site for sale, and they take 15% of the sale price.

That 15% definitely hurts, but to know that you can list your site and get it sold quickly 19 times out of 20 makes that 15% easier to swallow.

Their formula for selling a site is very simple:

Monthly Profit over the last 3-12 months X (20-30). Whether it's closer to 20 or closer to 30 depends on a handful of factors such as how long you've been in business, how many hours of work are required on the new owner's part when he/she takes over, how big your email list is, how much traffic you get, and so on.

Standard businesses sell for 60 times monthly profit, so that 20-30 figure also stings. But if you know you want to sell your site and move it out the door quickly, freeing up a nice wad to pour into other, more promising projects of yours, then it might just be the right move.

So, for example, let's say my site Buck Books is earning $10,000 per month in profit. I can sell it through Empire Flippers for $200,000-300,000 minus 15% for a total payout of $170,000-255,000. If the monthly profit is increasing and it's not taking up any of my time, it might be dumb to sell it for only 20-30 times monthly profit.

However, if I have a better business that could stand to benefit from a sudden injection of $250,000, it might be a wiser move. Also, selling a website, from a tax standpoint, is like selling an asset. In the U.S., we're taxed 15-20% for capital gains typically, which might be less than half of the normal tax rate on a business making $10,000 in monthly profits.

Yes, lots of factors to consider, and there aren't always clear answers as to what is the right and wrong move, but I personally lean on the side of collecting a large chunk of money all at once.

Are you the type that has flurries of obsessive excitement about certain subjects and ideas, but your interest often fizzles after a few months to a year when the next big thing comes along? Site-flipping might be something to consider. I mean, if you can just get a site making a consistent profit of $2,000 per month by the end of the first year, you should be able to sell it and pocket $50,000, having yourself a pretty nice year. Then, you've got a nice, clean start to try it again with your next fetish, and you've got a hefty 50,000-gallon tank of website jet fuel to help you do even better in the next round.

If you're even more spastically scatterbrained and can't even stay focused on building a site for a full year, you can flip them ever faster for smaller amounts at Flippa.com.

Anyway, I'm starting to get into bullshit territory again, as I haven't actually sold a site. Just researched it and thought about it all the way to the point of getting on the phone with people from Empire Flippers. But I got cold feet. Letting go of something that's making a profit every month that you built from a little photon cloud inside your brain is easier said than done. But someday I shall pull the trigger and see what it's like to get a couple years' profit all in one check.

Well folks, I'm a real human, and as any real human that's written a book can tell you, it gets exciting when you get close to the end. Those final chapters are often really short! I'm dying to sum this thing up, leave you with an optimistic outlook on your own online earning potential (hopefully you're there already), and tell you our plans for serving this wonderful community of individuals looking to break out of the traditional workforce mold and start making their friends and family members jealous. Alright then, let's do it...

CONCLUSION

How has reading this book up to this point affected you? Does the path to earning an internet-based income not seem more clear to you now, and more doable? We certainly hope it does. We've tried to do everything in our power to remove the intimidation and mystery of making money online. While we don't want to fall into the camp of air-headed cheerleaders that reassure EVERYONE that they can do it, we do know that with an "I got this" attitude, a decent idea, a fairly realistic plan for implementing that idea and growing it, and determination to break through the difficult digital Freshman phase that is filled with mistakes and disappointment (virtual wedgies and swirlies aplenty), that most can indeed achieve a digitally-free lifestyle.

We have just a few final tips to share before we send you on your way to plot and plan your escape!

1. **Don't let your emotions guide you in the early going.** Daydreaming of a freedom-filled future is really exciting—a little TOO exciting—and it can lead to becoming irrationally elated with outrageously high expectations, which is a recipe for heartbreaking letdown. Being successful online is like learning any other skill. The learning part is difficult, daunting, frustrating, and even humiliating at times. If you take happily-ever-after expectations into it, that completely unglamorous, unrewarding process

of slaving in front of the screen for endless hours, trying to figure out what went wrong and how to fix it, might just bum you out so much that you give up. Do yourself a favor and be sure to buckle up your emotional seatbelt before you press on the gas pedal. A wise man once said, "Nothing is ever as good or bad as it seems." We distort and exaggerate reality with our emotions, and if we let them guide us, we are letting the distorted and exaggerated version of the truth (irrationality) be our guide through life. You'll never succeed that way. Expect to be faced with great challenges and failures when you start, and be prepared to face them with courage and determination. You do that, and you'll make it past the difficult early stages that kill 95%+ of people's attempts to earn a full-time internet-based income.

2. **Be true to yourself.** One of the most common mistakes in life is trying hard to be something that you're not. You really need to identify who you are, what your natural gifts, talents, and interests are, and what you like doing. Then make sure your idea for earning a dependable living online is in alignment with that. If you hate writing, don't try to make a living with self-publishing just because so and so is crushing it and you wish you were, too. Don't make videos about celebrity gossip if what you really love is gardening just because gossip videos are more popular. You'll always get farther in life and be the most successful doing something you love and are naturally gifted at whether it seems to make sense as a business or not. That's because if you love it you'll do it more and do it better, and what you work harder on and are better at is always going to lead to more value to someone else in the long run. Besides, becoming digitally free by doing something you don't like isn't "freedom" at all. Dream big and shoot

for the ultimate outcome—making money doing what you love. Anything less will fail to satisfy you.

3. **Keep things as simple as possible.** People starting out often try to mimic what others are doing, and they immediately jump online and try to blog, write a book, create a course, create an autoresponder series, start a podcast, run ads, start a YouTube channel, put together a big online summit, stay active on Facebook, Twitter, Instagram, Pinterest, Snapchat, LinkedIn, Quora, Slideshare, and Medium, and the list goes on. It's madness. Absolute madness. To be successful online you just need to find **one** strategy that works and do that over and over again. You don't need to do EVERY strategy. A successful online business can be as simple as creating a system that acquires email subscribers through just one method for $2.50 each that makes an average of $5 in revenue per subscriber. No complications necessary. The less experienced you are, the more important simplicity becomes.

4. **Don't listen to your friends and family.** Unless your friends and family members are successful internet entrepreneurs, don't listen to them. They'll likely tell you to "get a real job" and try to make you feel like you are being naïve for trying to make a living online. Most people have had hard lives and have next to nothing to show for it. It makes them uncomfortable to think that they could have made great money doing something they loved and avoided $100,000 of student loan debt and decades of miserable indentured servitude at their jobs. They have little else to take pride in other than their ability to withstand suffering. The possibility of "digital freedom" sounds like a money-for-nothing pipedream to them. For those with a strong vision and determination to achieve digital freedom, it's no naïve pipedream. It's real, and it can

become real pretty quickly. Always make sure the volume of the voices inside your head (your vision, your dream) is louder than the voices on the outside. Seek advice only from those who have achieved what you are trying to achieve. Ignore advice from those who haven't.

5. **Be prepared, but not underprepared or overprepared.** One of the most common failure stories in internet business is the story of the entitled person who thinks they can go in unprepared, guns-a-blazin', and wreck the internet. The other most common failure story is the "course collector" who reads 100 books and spends $10,000 on courses that hasn't earned a single dollar online. You know the type. It's extremely common. It's the type who goes to graduate school, not because they want to learn more, but because they are afraid to actually get out into the real world and make something happen. Are you one of these types? If so, know your tendency and do something to break the pattern!

And on that note, the last thing you need from us right now is a longer list of things to be mindful of! While there's clearly a lot to starting from scratch and getting all the way to a reliable full-time living coming in exclusively from the internet, there's no real way to learn how to do it other than to actually do it. Those who try to learn everything before they do anything never start!

That doesn't mean that you won't need to educate yourself before and during the process, or that you can make it from zero to hero without any support at all. You need lots of both. We know that as well as anyone, as both Hung and I studied hard and had a variety of mentors before we ever made enough money to comfortably cut ties with the world of employment. And we, along with the rest of the

Digital Freedom Academy team (Steve Reed, Adam Bailey, Josh Driver, and Jonatas Botelho—and our comrade Todd Dosenberry at Digital Freedom Live), are here to provide what you need to the best of our ability.

This book is a great start, but we've got a lot more in store for you to get you where you want to go...

ABOUT DIGITAL FREEDOM ACADEMY

By Matt Stone

In the spring of 2015 I got the idea of inviting top experts to put together specific eCourses on niche topics pertaining to home-based business, and hosting them all on one site. I summed up this vision by calling it a "Udemy for home-based business."

If you're not familiar with Udemy, it's a huge hub of eCourses on any and every subject you can imagine. Courses are typically listed in the $20-399 range, but Udemy runs sales all the time. You can pretty much snag whatever course you want over there for $19 each, as long as you are patient enough to wait for a sale.

The problem with Udemy is that any Joe Schmo (or scammer) can put together a course and sell it. Sure, Udemy has reviews and things to help their users avoid purchasing garbage, but as with any platform that relies on reviews, it's an easy thing for hackers to hack. There is no procuring for quality. Anyone can sign up for an account and upload a "course" over there, and since it's generally a bad business idea to sell a course on a big platform as opposed to your own site, you can be sure that even the highest-rated courses on Udemy weren't made by the true experts.

I mean, one very successful Udemy instructor made a video boasting about how he makes $30,000 per month from his

Udemy courses. Sounds impressive, but he had made like 20+ courses to get there. Like I mentioned earlier, I made $40,000 with the first course launch I did in the first week—before I even created it! And then $70,000 with the second course launch in the first month. I know plenty of people who've made 7-figures in a week with a course launch. Guess what, none of them were hosted on Udemy! Hell no. Udemy is generally a place where you can pay to get "educated" by amateurs. It's no place for an aspiring internet entrepreneur to be trying to learn the ropes. The only ropes you'll find over there will be tied around your hands and feet, keeping you from getting anywhere.

Rather, I wanted to host things like a podcasting course by Pat Flynn, a self-publishing course by Steve Scott, and so on. I'm talking about really awesome courses by the best of the best experts and educators, and no filler at all.

I mean, I'm searching through Udemy right now for courses about YouTube. I quit after finding 200. I'm sure there are over 1,000. Really what people need is one, great, thorough, definitive course from a real expert on how to be successful on YouTube. 200+ courses on the same thing? That's utter madness.

So quickly I dropped the whole idea of making a "Udemy for home-based business." Udemy is not a great service. It's a blinding orgy of amateur slop. I want to create something *much better* than that. Something that doesn't already exist. And not only do I want it to be as affordable as Udemy, I want to obliterate Udemy on price. I want to shock and awe people by providing the best content at the lowest price. I want to make the impossible, possible. I want it all.

And so the vision for Digital Freedom Academy has continued to evolve. We now plan to offer courses on as many niche home-based business topics as possible. We also plan to offer dozens and dozens of outstanding books. In addition to that we'll have exclusive interviews with leading experts, create an amazing, supportive community with boundless networking opportunities, host live, in-person events and workshops, and eventually even offer a variety of in-house tools, software, and services once we've really got things cranking.

The supply of resources we make available won't be static either. We'll be constantly hunting down the best books, courses, tools, and resources that we can get our mitts on, and adding fresh, cutting-edge content to the platform every single week.

It all starts in mid-November of 2016. Before then, you can sign up to receive updates about when things go live at our homepage: www.digitalfreedom.academy

There won't be any annoying upsells to get premium content. You won't have to choose between eight different blogging courses and hope you get lucky and pick the right one. Nothing like that. We're doing something much better than that…

ALL educational resources on the site will be available to EVERYONE.

The general public will be able to sample everything on the entire platform for up to two weeks COMPLETELY FREE with no payment information required or any of that annoying crap to check it out. After that, if you want to continue to access the materials as well as any and all future materials that we add to the site (new stuff each week, like I said), you can do so at an amazingly low price—$19.99 per month, $199 annually, or $299 for lifetime access. This is literally less expensive than the current going price of a really good eCourse. Just one!

Building this, and convincing true experts with quality books and courses to host their content on Digital Freedom Academy, is a monumental undertaking. We've got our work cut out for us to put it lightly. This is bigger and more complex than any undertaking we as a team have ever tried to take on.

But we really want to bring this to the global community of freedom seekers out there. We've been in your shoes, and the strong desires for digital freedom make you the most easily-exploitable group of people on earth. The promise of making money and doing so without having to go to work is so strong in so many people that the jackals are waiting at every corner for you to open up your wallet. The fact that one of the most successful internet business educators on earth has NEVER STARTED AN INTERNET BUSINESS (other than her business to help people learn about internet business!) and charges $2,000 for her course, just goes to show how easy it is to prey upon the unhappily employed.

We want to be the good guys, with your best interests at heart, and scratching, clawing, and biting to fight for good resources at a price that's reasonable for just about anyone in any country on earth with a strong desire to free themselves. Yes, it will be a fight. We're even calling ourselves "Freedom Fighters." But I truly believe that there are others out there that share our ethic, and will be honored to be part of it by sharing their best content with DFA members.

We want to help you, but we need your help, too. If you are reading this book before November 2016, you can play a part in helping this vision come to life. We need to raise funds to launch this successfully—to put a half dozen of our other sites practically on hold for several months while we focus 110% on procuring our first round of resources.

And so we're launching our exclusive pre-release DFA Charter Membership for our first 1,000 backers.

These memberships are only $99 and will give you LIFE-TIME access to all the educational materials we host on the platform. That's but *one third* of the $299 price tag for lifetime access once we go live in November.

In addition to lifetime access, we're promising a 50% discount to attend our very first live, in-person event that we project to go down in early 2018 in some really cool place.

If you are seeking digital freedom, you need this, and we have the passion, drive, and experience to bring it to you. Sign up now to be one of our founding members, and help us make Digital Freedom Academy everything we want it to be.

To do that, simply go to: digitalfreedom.academy/charter and get signed up before the 1,000 slots are filled.

If you're reading this book after November of 2016, come check it out! www.DigitalFreedom.Academy.

Best of luck in your quest for freedom, and thanks for reading,

Hung Pham and Matt Stone

August, 2016

Made in the USA
Middletown, DE
15 December 2016